CONTENTS

INSTANT VORTEX AIR FRYER OVEN OVERVIEW

The Instant Vortex Air Fryer Oven is a mid-sized air fryer designed to make cooking all your favorites quick and effortless! Delight in the rich flavor of deep frying, the health benefits of air frying, and the same reliability and convenience you've come to expect from other Instant Brands products. This wonder-fryer allows you to Air Fry, Roast, Broil, Bake, Toast, Reheat, Proof, Dehydrate and Rotisserie cook your food, all with one touch!

The Vortex makes it easy and fun for anyone — from beginners to pros — to prepare healthy, tasty meals, fast. Air fryers use hot air, rather than hot oil, to produce the same crispy crunchy taste and texture that makes deep fried food so delectable. The blast of hot air traps all that juicy moisture beneath the crispy coating, but air fryers are quicker, cleaner, healthier, and a whole lot easier than deep fryers.

The oven's control panel is bright, easy to read and even easier to use. For total control over cooking, customize the cooking time and temperature so your favorite meals can be made the way you like them with one simple touch.

COOKING TIMETABLE

Food	Setting	Cook Time*	Temperature*	Accessory and Placement
Thin-cut fries (Frozen)	Air Fry / Roast	14 – 18 minutes	400°F / 205°C	Rotisserie Basket
Thin-cut fries (Fresh)	Air Fry / Roast	18 - 20 minutes	400°F / 205°C	Rotisserie Basket
Thick-cut fries (Frozen)	Air Fry / Roast	16 - 20 minutes	400°F / 205°C	Rotisserie Basket
Thick-cut fries (Fresh)	Air Fry / Roast	20 - 25 minutes	400°F / 205°C	Rotisserie Basket
Chicken wings	Air Fry / Roast	20 - 30 minutes	360°F / 182°C	Cooking Tray, Bottom / Rotisserie Basket
Whole chicken (up to 4 lbs)	Roast	55 - 60 minutes	380°F / 193°C	Rotisserie Spit
Chicken nuggets (Frozen)	Broil	10 - 15 minutes	400°F / 205°C	Cooking Tray, Middle
Shrimp (Frozen)	Air Fry	8 minutes	400°F / 205°C	Cooking Tray, Middle / Rotisserie Basket
Shrimp (Fresh)	Air Fry	8 - 10 minutes	350°F / 177°C	Cooking Tray, Middle / Rotisserie Basket
Fish sticks (Frozen)	Broil	8 - 12 minutes	400°F / 205°C	Cooking Tray, Middle
Asparagus	Broil / Bake	7 - 9 minutes	370°F / 188°C	Cooking Tray, Middle / Rotisserie Basket
Cauliflower	Broil / Bake	6 - 10 minutes	370°F / 188°C	Cooking Tray, Middle / Rotisserie Basket
Cake	Bake	25 – 35 minutes	360°F / 182°C	Drip Pan, Bottom (Springform Pan)
Dough	Proof	25 – 35 minutes	90ºF / 32°C	Drip Pan, Middle (place ½ cup water in an ovensafe container in the cooking chamber)
Fruit Leather	Dehydrate	8 – 12 hours	140ºF / 60°C	Drip Pan, Middle / Bottom
Beef Jerky	Dehydrate	3 – 5 hours	175 ºF / 80°C	Cooking Tray, Middle

*Cook times and temperatures are recommendations only. Always follow a trusted recipe.

COOKING TIPS:

Instant air fryer ovens cook all your favorite fresh and frozen oven-baked and deep-fried snacks—fast!

• Use the preset Smart Programs as a starting point, and experiment with cooking times and temperatures to get the results you prefer.

• Rotisserie-cooked foods and rotisserie accessories must be placed in the oven before touching Start.

• With the exception of rotisserie-cooked foods, most foods benefit greatly from a preheated oven. Wait for the display to read Add Food before inserting food into the cooking chamber.

• When cooking coated food items, choose breadcrumb batters over liquid- based batters to ensure that the batter sticks to the food.

• For crispy, golden fries, soak fresh potato sticks in ice water for 15 minutes, then pat dry and spray with cooking oil before adding them to the air fryer oven.

• When baking cakes, pies, quiches, or any food with filling or batter, use an oven-safe baking dish and cover food with foil or an oven-safe lid to prevent the top from overcooking.

• The drip pan doubles as a flat cooking tray. Use the drip pan when cooking fragile or filled food.

• When cooking pizza, insert both cooking trays into the oven and place the pizza on the bottom cooking tray.

• Pat moist food items dry before cooking to prevent smoke, splatter and excess steam.

• Air frying can cause oil and fat to drip from foods. To prevent excess smoke, carefully remove and empty the drip pan periodically throughout cooking.

• To ensure seasoning adheres properly, spray food items with cooking oil before adding seasoning.

• All oven-safe cookware is safe to use in the air fryer oven.

CARE AND CLEANING

Clean your Instant Vortex Pro air fryer oven and accessories after each use. Always unplug the oven and let it cool to room temperature before cleaning. Let all surfaces dry thoroughly before use, and before storage.

Part / Accessory	Instruction	Cleaning Method
Rotisserie Basket	For best results, use a bristled brush rather than a sponge or cloth. Optionally, spray with non-stick cooking spray before adding food.	Dishwasher or Hand Wash
Rotisserie Spit and Forks	Disassemble before cleaning after each use.	
Cooking Trays	Do not cover cooking trays when cooking. Air must be able to circulate freely. Cooking trays have a non-stick coating. Avoid using metal utensils when cleaning.	
Rotisserie Lift	Clean as needed.	
Drip Pan	Remove for cleaning and ensure all grease and food debris is fully removed. Optionally, line the pan with aluminum foil or parchment paper for easier cleaning.	
Cooking Chamber	Clean the cooking chamber walls as needed. Always check the heating coil for food debris and clean the heating coil as needed. Ensure the heating coil is dry before turning on the air fryer oven.	Damp Cloth Only
Removable Door	Allow to air dry completely before reinstalling.	
Outer Body and Stainless Steel	Clean with a soft, damp cloth or sponge, and wipe dry to avoid streaking.	

*Some discoloration of parts may occur after machine washing. This will not affect the safety nor the performance of the cooker.

Note: To remove baked-on grease residue from accessories and the cooking chamber, spray the affected area with a mixture of baking soda and vinegar, and wipe clean with a damp cloth. For stubborn stains, allow the mixture to sit on the affected area for several minutes before scrubbing clean.

Remove the Oven Door

1. Place one hand on top of the air fryer oven to hold it firmly in place.
2. Open the oven door to a 45º angle from the oven.
3. Pull the oven door up from the right side until it pops out of its track.

Reinstall the Oven Door

1. Hold the oven door at a 45º angle from the oven.
2. Align the teeth at the bottom of the oven door with the grooves in the air fryer oven.
3. Press down on the right side of the oven door until it pops into place, then press the left side down.

20 BEST AIR FRYER OVEN RECIPES

ISLAND SCALLOPS

4 Servings

Ingredients

- 1 can coconut milk
- 15 ounce Pineapple juice
- 3 teaspoon   Sea Salt
- 2 tablespoon rum
- 1.25 pound   sea scallops
- 2 cup   pineapple cubed
- 0.5 cup   coconut flakes
- papaya diced
- avocado diced
- Red onion diced
- lime squeezed
- 2 tablespoon Extra Virgin Olive Oil
- 0.25 teaspoon black pepper
- 0.25 teaspoon salt
- 0.25 cup cilantro

Directions

1. Combine the coconut milk, pineapple juice, sea salt and rum in a large bowl.
2. Soak the sea scallops in the mixture.
3. Combine ingredients for salsa and set aside.
4. Assemble skewers alternating the scallops and pineapple chunks.
5. Place skewers into rotisserie holder.
6. Place into Instant Vortex Air Fryer Oven. Set time for 10 min. Set temperature for 400 degrees. Press the rotisserie button.
7. Serve with salsa.

SHRIMP PO' BOY

4 Servings

Ingredients

- 0.5 teaspoon Garlic powder
- 0.5 teaspoon onion powder
- 1 teaspoon   salt
- 0.25 teaspoon cayenne pepper
- 1 teaspoon Paprika
- 1 cup buttermilk
- large egg, beaten
- 1 cup   flour
- 0.5 cup   cornmeal
- 16   shrimp, peeled, deveined & tails removed
- 0.5 cup   mayonnaise
- 2 tablespoon chili sauce
- 4   Portuguese rolls
- lettuce, shredded
- tomatoes, sliced
- dill pickle slices

Directions

1. Combine the seasoning ingredients in a bowl.
2. Combine the egg mixture ingredients in a second bowl.
3. Combine the cornmeal mixture ingredients in a third bowl.
4. Toss the shrimp in the bowl with the seasoning to coat the shrimp in the seasoning, then dip the shrimp in the bowl with the egg mixture, and finally coat the shrimp in the cornmeal mixture.
5. Place the shrimp on two Air Flow Racks. Spray the shrimp with the olive oil spray. Place the Racks on the middle and upper shelves of the Instant Vortex Air Fryer Oven.
6. Press the Power Button, increase the cooking temperature to 390° F, and decrease the cooking time 12 mins. Rotate the Racks halfway through the cooking time (6 mins.).
7. Combine the sauce ingredients in a bowl.
8. Spread the sauce on the Portuguese rolls and place the lettuce, tomato, and pickles on the rolls.
9. Top the rolls with the shrimp.

TURKEY GUACAMOLE BURGER

4 Servings

Ingredients

- 1 pound Ground turkey
- 0.5 cup diced canned tomatoes, liquid drained
- jalapeno, seeded & minced
- 2 teaspoon cilantro, chopped
- 2 tablespoon breadcrumbs, plain
- 1 teaspoon salt
- avocados, crushed
- 0.5 small red onion, chopped finely
- 2 tablespoon cilantro, chopped
- 0.5 plum tomato, diced small
- 2 teaspoon Lime juice
- 0.75 teaspoonsalt
- hamburger buns
- 0.25 cup margarine
- 0.5 cup queso fresco, crumbled

Directions

1. Combine the burger ingredients in a bowl. Shape the combined ingredients into four patties.

2. Mix the guacamole ingredients in another bowl until the guacamole is creamy.

3. Place the burgers on an Air Flow Rack. Place the Rack on the middle shelf of the Instant Vortex Air Fryer Oven.

4. Press the Power Button and increase the cooking temperature to 390° F and the cooking time to 20 mins. Flip the burgers halfway through the cooking time (10 mins.).

5. Set the burgers aside.

6. Cut the hamburger buns in half horizontally and butter them with the margarine.

7. Place two buns on an Air Flow Rack. Place the Rack on the middle shelf of the Instant Vortex Air Fryer Oven.

8. Press the Power Button and cook until the rolls are golden (about 3 mins.). Repeat until all the buns are toasted.

9. Place the burgers on the buns with the guacamole and the queso fresco.

MOJITO LAMB KABOBS

4 Servings

Ingredients

- 4 Limes, divided
- 0.5 cup Extra Virgin Olive Oil
- 0.25 cup fresh mint, chopped
- 8 large cloves garlic, minced
- 2 teaspoon salt
- 0.5 teaspoon pepper
- 12 lamb loin chops, trimmed

Directions

1. In a large bowl, combine the zest and juice from 3 limes, oil, mint, garlic, salt and pepper; mix well.

2. Add the lamb and toss to coat.

3. Marinate the lamb for 4 hours, tossing every hour.

4. Cut the remaining lime into wedges.

5. Skewer the meaty part of 2 lamb chops onto a skewer. Place a lime wedge onto the skewer and repeat with two additional pieces of lamb, another wedge and a final two pieces of lamb.

6. Make a second skewer.

7. Drape the bones of the first skewer over the center spit and attach the skewer to the rotisserie wheel.

8. Use an empty skewer to secure the lamb bones.

9. Rotate the wheel and repeat with the second lamb skewer.

10. Roast at 370 for 15-20 minutes for medium-rare.

BRATWURST & PICKLE KABOBS

5 Servings

Ingredients

- 4   fully cooked bratwurst cut into 1 inch medallions
- 4   dill pickles cut into 1/2 inch medallions
- 20   pretzel nuggets, thawed
- 0.25 cup pretzel salt
- Spicy Mustard for serving

Directions

1. Place 5 bratwurst medallions and 4 pickle medallions onto a skewer of a Instant Vortex Air Fryer Oven, alternating the meat and pickles.

2. Make 4 more meat and pickle skewers.

3. Skewer 4 pretzel nuggets onto a skewer.

4. Brush water over the nuggets and sprinkle with some pretzel salt.

5. Make 4 more pretzel skewers.

6. Clip the skewers onto the skewer attachment, alternating skewers of pretzels and meat.

7. Cook for 10 minutes at 350 degrees. 8. Serve hot with spicy mustard.

HARVEST GRANOLA

16 Servings

Ingredients

- 1.66667 cup   sliced almonds
- 1 cup   rolled oats
- 0.5 cup   pumpkin seeds
- 1.5 teaspoon   salt
- 1 teaspoon   Canola Oil
- 0.333333 cup maple syrup
- 1 cup   Dried Cranberries

Directions

1. Combine the almonds, oats, pumpkin seeds, sunflower seeds and salt; mix.

2. Add the oil and syrup.

3. Toss to combine.

4. Place parchment onto 3 Instant Vortex Air Fryer trays.

5. Sprinkle the granola mixture evenly over the trays.

6. Bake at 220 for 40 minutes, rotating the trays hallway through the cooking time.
7. Add the cranberries and toss to combine.
8. Cool.

BOURBON GLAZED PINEAPPLE

8 Servings

Ingredients

- Pineapple, top and bottom removed, skin removed
- 2 tablespoon bourbon
- 2 tablespoon Brown Sugar
- 2 tablespoon melted butter
- 0.5 teaspoon Vanilla Extract

Directions

1. Place the pineapple on the spit of a Instant Vortex Air Fryer Oven and secure with the fork attachments.
2. In a small bowl, combine the bourbon, brown sugar, melted butter and vanilla extract; stir.
3. Roast the pineapple at 400 degrees for 40 minutes, brushing with the bourbon glaze every 5 minutes.
4. Make sure to push the rotate button.
5. Remove the pineapple from the spit and slice.
6. Serve with ice cream, whipped cream, chopped pecans and a drizzle of caramel sauce.

FRENCH ONION KALE CHIPS

2 Servings

Ingredients

- 1 bunch kale, stems removed and ripped into chunks
- 2 tablespoon Extra Virgin Olive Oil
- 2 tablespoon French onion soup mix

Directions

1. Place the kale in a large bowl.
2. Drizzle the olive oil over the kale and toss well until all pieces are coated.
3. Sprinkle the French onion soup mix powder over the kale and toss well to coat.
4. Spread the kale in a single layer onto the trays of a Instant Vortex Air Fryer Oven.

5. Dehydrate at 125 degrees for 2 hours.

GINGER CRANBERRY SCONES

8 Servings

Ingredients

- 2.75 cup all-purpose flour
- 0.25 cup dark brown sugar
- 1.5 teaspoon Baking Powder
- 1.5 teaspoon cinnamon
- 0.5 teaspoon freshly ground nutmeg
- 0.25 teaspooncloves
- 1 teaspoon salt
- 0.5 cup Dried Cranberries
- 10 tablespoon unsalted butter, frozen, grated on a box grater
- 0.5 cup heavy cream, plus more for glazing
- 1 teaspoon Canola Oil
- large egg
- 1 teaspoon Vanilla Extract
- 0.25 cup sour cream
- Demerara sugar, for sprinkling

Directions

1. Combine the flour, sugar, baking powder, baking soda, cinnamon, nutmeg, cloves, salt, ginger and cranberries in a large bowl. Mix to combine.
2. Add the butter and toss.
3. In a separate bowl, combine the heavy cream, oil, egg, vanilla and sour cream; whisk until smooth.
4. Add the wet ingredients to the dry and stir to form a thick dough.
5. Shape dough into a circle a ¾" in thickness.
6. Cut into 8 wedges
7. Brush the tops with heavy cream and top with a sprinkling of demerara sugar.
8. Place on 2 Air Fryer Oven air flow trays.
9. Bake for 12 minutes at 365 degrees, rotate trays and bake an additional 6 minutes at 365 degrees.

PHILLY CHEESESTEAK STUFFED BREAD

6 Servings

Ingredients

- 0.5 pound   thinly sliced top round, sautéed and cooled
- 2   medium white onions, sliced caramelized, and cooled
- 2 cup   American cheese, shredded
- Salt and Pepper
- round crusty loaf of bread

Directions

1. In a large bowl, combine the top round, caramelized onions and ½ cups of the cheese; mix well.
2. Season the mixture with salt and pepper, to taste.
3. Using a serrated knife, cut 1" slices into the bread, but do not cut all the way through.
4. Rotate the bread 90 degrees, and cut 1" slices in the same manner to create squares.
5. Gently fan the bread and jam the stuffing into the cavities until all filling is used.
6. Sprinkle the remaining American cheese over the top.
7. Bake on a Instant Vortex Air Fryer Oven tray for 6 minutes at 375 degrees.

EVERYTHING BAGEL SNACK MIX

8 Servings

Ingredients

- 1 cup   square rice cereal
- 1 cup   square corn cereal
- 1 cup   cheese squares
- 1 cup   mixed nuts
- 1 cup   bite-sized pretzels
- 1 cup   bagel chips, broken into pieces
- 3 tablespoon butter, melted
- 1 tablespoon Worcestershire sauce
- 1 tablespoon everything bagel spice
- 0.25 cup Sesame seeds
- 0.25 cup poppy seeds
- 0.25 cup dried onion flakes
- 1.5 tablespoon   coarse sea salt

- 2 tablespoon dried garlic flakes

Directions

1. Combine the cereal, cheese squares, mixed nuts, pretzels, toast, and bagel chips in a bowl and mix.
2. Combine the Worcestershire sauce, everything bagel spice, sesame seeds, poppy seeds, onion flakes, salt, and garlic flakes in a separate bowl and mix.*
3. Line three air flow racks with parchment paper. Evenly divide the cereal mixture between the air flow racks. Evenly coat the cereal mixture with the spice mixture.
4. Place the air flow racks in the Instant Vortex Air Fryer Oven. Set the cooking time to 300° F and the cooking time to 15 mins.
5. When the cooking time is complete, remove the air flow racks from the Instant Vortex Air Fryer Oven and let the snack mix cool completely.
6. Any leftover spice mixture can be stored in an airtight container for up to 3 months.

PORK MILANESE WITH SPINACH AND CHEESE STUFFED MUSHROOMS

4 Servings

Ingredients

- 2   eggs, beaten
- 1.5 cup   seasoned breadcrumbs
- 4   thin-sliced boneless pork chops
- 4 ounce   cream cheese
- 0.5 cup   sour cream
- 1.5 cup   baby spinach, chopped
- 0.5 teaspoon Garlic powder
- 0.5 teaspoon salt
- 0.25 teaspoonpepper
- 4   medium-sized Portobello caps
- 0.5 cup   mozzarella, shredded

Directions

Set up a dredging station with the egg and breadcrumb. 2. Dip the pork chops into the egg and then into the breadcrumbs to coat. 3. Place the pork onto a Instant Vortex Air Fryer Oven tray. 4. Cook at 370 for 12 minutes, flipping halfway through the cooking time. For Mushrooms 1. Combine the cream cheese, sour cream, spinach, garlic powder, salt and pepper and mix to combine. 2. Remove the stalk from the mushrooms. 3. Fill the cavities with the cheese filling. 4.

Top with the mozzarella. 5. Place the mushroom caps onto a Instant Vortex Air Fryer Oven tray. 6. Bake at 370 for 12 minutes.

CHICKEN MILANESE

2 Servings

Ingredients

- 2 cup   panko breadcrumbs
- 0.25 cup parmesan, grated
- 1 teaspoon   Garlic powder
- 4   chicken cutlets
- salt and black pepper, divided
- eggs, beaten
- 1 teaspoon   White wine vinegar
- juice of 1/2 lemon
- 2 tablespoon Extra Virgin Olive Oil
- 3 cup   arugula
- beefsteak tomato, diced
- shaved parmesan, for garnish

Directions

1. Combine panko breadcrumbs, Parmesan, and garlic powder in a bowl.
2. Generously season the chicken cutlets with the salt and pepper.
3. Add the eggs to a separate bowl.
4. Dip the cutlets into the egg. Then, coat with them the panko mixture.
5. Place the cutlets on the Air Flow Racks.
6. Press the Steaks/Chops Button (370° F). Decrease the cooking time to 15 minutes to begin cooking cycle.
7. While chicken cooks, make the salad: Whisk together the vinegar, lemon juice, olive oil, and a pinch of salt and pepper in a bowl.
8. Add the arugula and coat with the dressing.
9. When the chicken is done cooking, plate the chicken and top with the diced tomato and the arugula salad and garnish with the shaved Parmesan.

WHITE PIZZA

1 Servings

Ingredients

- thin-crust pizza dough
- 2 tablespoon extra virgin olive oil, divided
- 0.25 cup ricotta cheese
- 9 slice   fresh mozzarella
- 2 clove   garlic, thinly sliced
- 1 teaspoon   red pepper flakes

Directions

1. Rub the pizza dough with 1 tbsp. olive oil. Roll the pizza dough out to fit on an Air Flow Rack. Place the pizza on the rack and slide the rack into the middle shelf of the Instant Vortex Air Fryer Oven.
2. Press the Power Button and then the French Fries Button (400° F/200° C). Manually set the cooking time to 10 minutes to begin cooking cycle. Halfway through the cooking time (5 mins.), flip the dough.
3. Remove the crust from the AirFryer Oven.
4. Top the crust with the ricotta, mozzarella, garlic, and red pepper flakes. Return the pizza to the Instant Vortex Air Fryer Oven.
5. Press the Power Button and then the French Fries Button (400° F/200° C). Manually set the cooking time to 6 minutes to begin cooking cycle. Cook until the cheese is melted.
6. Drizzle 1 tbsp. olive oil over the pizza before serving.

MARYLAND CRAB CAKES

12 Servings

Ingredients

- 1 teaspoon   garlic,minced
- 0.25 cup scallions, finely chopped
- 0.25 cup Celery, diced
- 2 tablespoon fresh parsley, chopped
- 1 tablespoon sweet chili sauce
- 1 teaspoon   seafood seasoning
- 1 teaspoon   salt

- 0.5 teaspoon ground black pepper
- 1 cup   cracker crumbs
- 1 pound Lump crab meat
- 1 cup   mayonnaise
- 1 tablespoon sweet pickle relish
- 1 tablespoon thai chili sauce
- 1 tablespoon Lemon juice
- 1 pinch   salt and pepper to season

Directions

1. In a large bowl, combine all breadcrumb ingredients except crab meat and cracker crumbs
2. Gently mix in crab meat and 1/4 cup of the cracker crumbs.
3. Spread the remaining crumbs on a work surface.
4. Form crab mixture into 12 equally sized balls.
5. Place the balls onto the crumbs to evenly coat and gently press to make a patty.
6. Refrigerate for 20 minutes.
7. Arrange crab cakes onto the Air Flow Racks.
8. Press the Steaks/Chops Button. Decrease the Timer to 20 minutes to begin cooking cycle.
9. While the crab cakes cook, make the dipping sauce: combine all ingredients and season with salt and pepper.
10. Serve crab cakes warm with dipping sauce.

PEPPERONI STUFFED MOZZARELLA PATTIES

12 Servings

Ingredients

- 1 pound whole milk mozzarella
- 24 slice   pepperoni
- 4   eggs beaten
- 2 cup   seasoned Italian breadcrumbs

Directions

1. Slice a block of mozzarella into 1/4 inch slices. Cut each slice in half.
2. Place two slices of pepperoni over half of the slices.
3. Create a cheese sandwich with the remaining halves of mozzarella, and press firmly to seal.

4. Set up a dredging station with the flour, eggs and breadcrumbs. Dip each mozzarella sandwich into the flour, then the egg, and then the breadcrumb. Re-dip each sandwich into the egg and then the breadcrumbs.
5. Spray the patties with cooking spray.
6. Cook the sandwiches in the Instant Vortex Air Fryer Oven or XL at 400 degrees for 6 minutes, flipping the patties halfway through the cooking process.

CORNED BEEF AND CABBAGE EGG ROLLS

12 Servings

Ingredients
- 12   egg roll wrappers
- 0.75 pound   corned beef, shredded
- 1.5 cup   stewed cabbage
- Spicy Mustard

Directions
1. Working with one egg roll wrapper at a time, place the wrapper with one corner of the wrapper facing you.
2. Use about 2 tbsp. shredded corned beef to create a small log in the center of the wrapper. Top the corned beef with 1 tbsp. shredded cabbage. Roll the egg roll wrapper corner closest to you over the filling and carefully tuck the wrapper to create an airtight seal.
3. Brush the remaining edges of the wrapper with water. Fold in each side of the wrapper and then roll the egg roll up to seal. Repeat until all the meat and cabbage are used up.
4. Place the egg rolls on an Air Flow Rack. Spray the rolls with cooking spray. Slide the rack into the middle shelf of the Instant Vortex Air Fryer Oven. Press the French Fries button (400° F), adjust the cooking time to 7 mins., and cook until golden brown.
5. When the egg rolls are done cooking, serve them warm with spicy mustard.

CLAMS OREGANATA

4 Servings

Ingredients
- 1 cup   unseasoned breadcrumbs
- 0.25 cup Parmesan cheese, grated
- 0.25 cup parsley, chopped

- 1 teaspoon   dried oregano
- 3 clove   garlic, minced
- 4 tablespoon butter, melted
- 2   dozen clams, shucked

Directions

1. In a medium-sized bowl, combine the breadcrumbs, Parmesan, parsley, oregano, garlic, lemon zest and melted butter. Mix to create crumbs.
2. Place a heaping tbsp of the crumb mixture onto the exposed clams.
3. Fill the Copper Chef cake insert or other pan with a cup of coarse sea salt. Nestle the clams in the salt and cook at 400 for 3 minutes.
4. Garnish with fresh parsley and lemon wedges.

GREEN BEAN CASSEROLE RICEBALLS

4 Servings

Ingredients

- 1 cup   sushi rice, cooked
- 2   14.5 ounce cans cut green beans, drained
- 0.25 cup cream of mushroom soup
- 0.5 cup   whole milk ricotta
- 1 cup   Mozzarella cheese
- 1 pinch   Salt and Pepper
- 2 cup   fried onions
- 2 cup   all-purpose flour
- 2   eggs, beaten

Directions

1. In a large bowl, combine the rice, green beans, cream of mushroom soup, ricotta and mozzarella.
2. Stir to combine. Season with salt and pepper, to taste. The filling should be on the slightly salty side.
3. Refrigerate at least 30 minutes. Meanwhile, set up the dredging station.
4. Put the fried onions in a plastic zip-top bag. Use your hands to break the onions into crumbs. Transfer to a shallow bowl.
5. Roll the rice mixture into balls, about the size of a billiard's ball.

6. Roll each ball in the flour, followed by the egg, and, lastly, the onion crumbs.
7. Cook in an Air Fryer at 380, until golden brown, about 8 minutes. Serve hot.

FISH TACOS

6 Servings

Ingredients

- 1 cup   flour
- 1 tablespoon Cornstarch
- salt, to taste, divided
- 1.5 cup   seltzer water, cold
- 10 ounce cod filet
- 1 teaspoon   ground white pepper
- 1 cup   panko breadcrumbs
- 0.5 cup   guacamole
- 6   flour tortillas
- 1 cup   coleslaw
- 0.5 cup   salsa
- lemon, cut into wedges
- 2 tablespoon cilantro, chopped

Directions

Tempura Batter

1. In a bowl: Add the flour, cornstarch, and salt.
2. Mix in the cold seltzer.
3. Mix all the ingredients together until smooth.

Tacos

1. Cut the cod filet into long 2-oz pieces and season them with the salt and white pepper.
2. In a pan: Add the panko breadcrumbs. Dip each piece of cod into the tempura batter. Then, dredge the cod in the panko breadcrumbs.
3. Place the breaded cod on the Air Flow Racks. Slide the racks into the Instant Vortex Air Fryer Oven.
4. Set the Instant Vortex Air Fryer Oven to the French Fries setting (400° F). Set the cooking time to 10 mins. Halfway through the cooking cycle, turn the fish sticks.
5. Once the cooking time is complete, remove the fish sticks.

Spread the guacamole on a tortilla. Place one fish stick in the tortilla and top with some coleslaw, salsa, and a squeeze of lemon. Top with chopped cilantro. Repeat until all the ingredients are used up. Fold the tacos before eating.

BREAKFAST AND BRUNCH RECIPES

LEMON VANILLA CUPCAKES WITH YOGURT FROST

Cooking Time: 25 minutes
Serves: 5

Ingredients:
- Lemon Frosting:
- 1 cup natural yogurt
- Sugar to taste
- 1 orange, juiced
- 1 tbsp orange zest
- 7 oz cream cheese
- Cake:
- 2 lemons, quartered
- ½ cup flour + extra for basing
- ¼ tsp salt
- 2 tbsp sugar
- 1 tsp baking powder
- 1 tsp vanilla extract
- 2 eggs
- ½ cup softened butter
- 2 tbsp milk

Directions
1. In a bowl, add the yogurt and cream cheese. Mix until smooth. Add the orange juice and zest; mix well. Gradually add the sweetener to your taste while stirring until smooth. Make sure the frost is not runny. Set aside.
2. For cup cakes: Place the lemon quarters in a food processor and process it until pureed. Add the baking powder, softened butter, milk, eggs, vanilla extract, sugar, and salt. Process again until smooth.

3. Preheat the Air Fryer to 400 F. Flour the bottom of 10 cupcake cases and spoon the batter into the cases ¾ way up. Place them in the Air Fryer and bake for 7 minutes. Once ready, remove and let cool. Design the cupcakes with the frosting.

ALMOND, CINNAMON BERRY OAT BARS

Cooking Time: 40 minutes
Serves: 10

Ingredients:
- 3 cups rolled oats
- ½ cup ground almonds
- ½ cup flour
- 1 tsp baking powder
- 1 tsp ground cinnamon
- 3 eggs, lightly beaten
- ½ cup canola oil
- ⅓ cup milk
- 2 tsp vanilla extract
- 2 cups mixed berries

Directions
1. Spray a baking pan that fits in your air fryer with cooking spray.
2. In a bowl, add oats, almonds, flour, baking powder and cinnamon into and stir well. In another bowl, whisk eggs, oil, milk, and vanilla.
3. Stir the wet ingredients gently into the oat mixture. Fold in the berries. Pour the mixture in the pan and place in the fryer. Cook for 30 minutes at 330 F. When ready, check if the bars are nice and soft.

CHEESY POTATO & SPINACH FRITTATA

Cooking Time: 35 minutes
Serves: 4

Ingredients:

- 3 cups potato cubes, boiled
- 2 cups spinach, chopped
- 5 eggs, lightly beaten
- ¼ cup heavy cream
- 1 cup grated mozzarella cheese
- ½ cup parsley, chopped
- Fresh thyme, chopped
- Salt and black pepper to taste

Directions
1. Spray the air fryer's basket with oil. Arrange the potatoes inside.
2. In a bowl, whisk eggs, cream, spinach, mozzarella, parsley, thyme, salt and pepper, and pour over the potatoes. Cook for 16 minutes at 400 F, until nice and golden.

THINY CAPRESE SANDWICH WITH SOURDOUGH BREAD

Cooking Time: 25 minutes
Serves: 2

Ingredients:
- 4 slices sourdough bread
- 2 tbsp mayonnaise
- 2 slices ham
- 2 lettuce leaves
- 1 tomato, sliced
- 2 slices mozzarella cheese
- Salt and black pepper to taste

Directions
1. On a clean board, lay the sourdough slices and spread with mayonnaise. Top 2 of the slices with ham, lettuce, tomato and mozzarella. Season with salt and pepper.
2. Top with the remaining two slices to form two sandwiches. Spray with oil and transfer to the air fryer. Cook for 14 minutes at 340 F, flipping once halfway through cooking. Serve hot!

CINNAMON MANGO BREAD

Cooking Time: 60 minutes
Serves: 8

Ingredients:
- ½ cup melted butter
- 1 egg, lightly beaten
- ½ cup brown sugar
- 1 tsp vanilla extract
- 3 ripe mango, mashed
- 1 ½ cups plain flour
- 1 tsp baking powder
- ½ tsp grated nutmeg
- ½ tsp ground cinnamon

Directions
1. Spray a loaf tin, that fits in the air fryer, with cooking spray and line with baking paper. In a bowl, whisk melted butter, egg, sugar, vanilla and mango. Sift in flour, baking powder, nutmeg and cinnamon and stir without overmixing.
2. Pour the batter into the tin and place it the air fryer. Cook for 35 minutes at 300 F. Make sure to check at the 20-25-minute mark. When ready, let cool before slicing it.

CREAMY MUSHROOM AND SPINACH OMELET

Cooking Time: 10 minutes
Serves: 2

Ingredients:
- 4 eggs, lightly beaten
- 2 tbsp heavy cream
- 2 cups spinach, chopped
- 1 cup chopped mushrooms
- 3 oz feta cheese, crumbled
- A handful of fresh parsley, chopped

- Salt and black pepper

Directions
1. Spray your air fryer basket with cooking spray. In a bowl, whisk eggs and until combined. Stir in spinach, mushrooms, feta, parsley, salt and pepper.
2. Pour into the basket and cook for 6 minutes at 350 F. Serve immediately with a touch of tangy tomato relish.

CHEDDAR CHEESE HASH BROWNS

Cooking Time: 25 minutes
Serves: 4

Ingredients:
- 4 russet potatoes, peeled, grated
- 1 brown onion, chopped
- 3 garlic cloves, chopped
- ½ cup grated cheddar cheese
- 1 egg, lightly beaten
- Salt and black pepper
- 3 tbsp finely thyme sprigs

Directions
1. In a bowl, mix with hands potatoes, onion, garlic, cheese, egg, salt, black pepper and thyme. Spray the fryer with cooking spray.
2. Press the hash brown mixture into the basket and cook for 9 minutes at 400 F., shaking once halfway through cooking. When ready, ensure the hash browns are golden and crispy.

CHERRY IN VANILLA ALMOND SCONES

Cooking Time: 30 minutes
Serves: 4

Ingredients:

- 2 cups flour
- ⅓ cup sugar
- 2 tsp baking powder
- ½ cup sliced almonds
- ¾ cup chopped cherries, dried
- ¼ cup cold butter, cut into cubes
- ½ cup milk
- 1 egg
- 1 tsp vanilla extract

Directions

1. Line air fryer basket with baking paper. Mix together flour, sugar, baking powder, almonds and dried cherries. Rub the butter into the dry ingredients with hands to form a sandy, crumbly texture. Whisk together egg, milk and vanilla extract.
2. Pour into the dry ingredients and stir to combine. Sprinkle a working board with flour, lay the dough onto the board and give it a few kneads. Shape into a rectangle and cut into squares. Arrange the squares in the air fryer's basket and cook for 14 minutes at 390 F. Serve immediately.

SWEET CARAMEL FRENCH TOAST

Cooking Time: 15 minutes
Serves: 3

Ingredients:
- 6 slices white bread
- 2 eggs
- ¼ cup heavy cream
- ⅓ cup sugar mixed with 1 tsp ground cinnamon
- 6 tbsp caramel
- 1 tsp vanilla extract

Directions

1. In a bowl, whisk eggs and cream. Dip each piece of bread into the egg and cream. Dip the bread into the sugar and cinnamon mixture until well-coated. On a clean board, lay the coated slices and spread three of the slices with about 2 tbsp of

caramel each, around the center.

2. Place the remaining three slices on top to form three sandwiches. Spray the air fryer basket with oil. Arrange the sandwiches into the fryer and cook for 10 minutes at 340 F, turning once halfway through cooking.

BACON EGG MUFFINS WITH CHIVES

Cooking Time: 30 minutes
Serves: 10

Ingredients:
- 10 eggs, lightly beaten
- 10 bacon rashers, cut into small pieces
- ½ cup chopped chives
- 1 brown onion, chopped
- 1 cup grated cheddar cheese
- Salt and black pepper

Directions
1. Spray a 10-hole muffin pan with cooking spray. In a bowl, add eggs, bacon, chives, onion, cheese, salt and pepper, and stir to combine. Pour into muffin pans and place inside the fryer. Cook for 12 minutes at 330 F, until nice and set.

HONEYED BANANA & HAZELNUT CUPCAKES

Cooking Time: 40 minutes
Serves: 6

Ingredients:
- ½ cup melted butter
- ½ cup honey
- 2 eggs, lightly beaten
- 4 ripe bananas, mashed
- 1 tsp vanilla extract
- 2 cups flour

- 1 tsp baking powder
- ½ tsp baking soda
- 1 tsp ground cinnamon
- ½ cup chopped hazelnuts
- ½ cup dark chocolate chips

Directions

1. Spray 10-hole muffin with oil spray. In a bowl, whisk butter, honey, eggs, banana and vanilla, until well-combine. Sift in flour, baking powder, baking soda and cinnamon without overmixing.
2. Stir in the hazelnuts and chocolate into the mixture. Pour the mixture into the muffin holes and place in the air fryer. Cook for 30 minutes at 350 F, checking them at the around 20-minute mark.

CRUNCHY CINNAMON TOAST STICKS

Cooking Time: 15 minutes
Serves: 3

Ingredients:

- 5 slices bread
- 3 eggs
- Salt and black pepper to taste
- 1 ½ tbsp butter
- ⅛ tsp cinnamon powder
- A pinch nutmeg powder
- A pinch clove powder

Directions

1. Preheat the Air Fryer to 350 F. In a bowl, add clove powder, eggs, nutmeg powder, and cinnamon powder. Beat well using a whisk. Season with salt and pepper. Use a bread knife to apply butter on both sides of the bread slices and cut them into 3 or 4 strips.
2. Dip each strip in the egg mixture and arrange them in one layer in the fryer's basket. Cook for 2 minutes. Once ready, pull out the fryer basket and spray the toasts with cooking spray. Flip the toasts and spray the other side with cooking

spray. Slide the basket back to the fryer and cook for 4 minutes. Check regularly to prevent them from burning. Once the toasts are golden brown, remove them onto a serving platter. Dust with cinnamon and serve with syrup.

BUTTERY SCRAMBLE EGGS

Cooking Time: 11 minutes
Serves: 2

Ingredients:
- 2 slices bread
- 2 eggs
- Salt and black pepper to taste
- 2 tbsp butter

Directions
1. Place a 3 X 3 cm heatproof bowl in the fryer's basket and brush with butter. Make a hole in the middle of the bread slices with a bread knife and place in the heatproof bowl in 2 batches.
2. Break an egg into the center of each hole. Season with salt and pepper. Close the Air Fryer and cook for 4 minutes at 330 F. Turn the bread with a spatula and cook for another 4 minutes.

PAPRIKA & PICKLES FRITTERS

Cooking Time: 15 minutes
Serves: 2

Ingredients:
- 8 medium pickles
- 1 egg, beaten
- ½ cup breadcrumbs
- 1 tsp paprika
- 4 tbsp flour
- 1 tbsp olive oil

- Salt, to taste

Directions

1. Preheat the Air fryer to 350 F and cut the pickles lengthwise; pat them dry. Combine the flour, paprika and salt, in a small bowl. In another bowl, combine the breadcrumbs and olive oil. Dredge in the flour first, dip them in the beaten egg, and then coat them with the crumbs. Arrange on a lined baking sheet and place in the Air fryer. Cook for 10 minutes.

CHEESY SAUSAGE EGG DISH

Cooking Time: 20 minutes
Serves: 6

Ingredients:
- 1 lb minced breakfast sausage
- 6 eggs
- 1 red pepper, diced
- 1 green pepper, diced
- 1 yellow pepper, diced
- 1 sweet onion, diced
- 2 cups Cheddar cheese, shredded
- Salt and black pepper to taste
- fresh parsley to garnish

Directions

1. Place a skillet over medium heat on a stove top, add the sausage and cook until brown, stirring occasionally. Once done, drain any excess fat derived from cooking and set aside.
2. Grease a casserole dish that fits into the fryer basket with cooking spray, and arrange the sausage on the bottom. Top with onion, red pepper, green pepper, and yellow pepper. Spread the cheese on top.
3. In a bowl, beat the eggs and season with salt and black pepper. Pour the mixture over the casserole. Place the casserole dish in the air basket, and bake at 355 F for 13-15 minutes. Serve warm garnished with fresh parsley.

VEGETARIAN RECIPES

POTATO GRATIN

Cooking Time: 20 minutes
Serves: 4

Ingredients:
- 2 large potatoes, sliced thinly
- 5½ tablespoons cream
- 2 eggs
- 1 tablespoon plain flour
- ½ cup cheddar cheese, grated

Directions:
1. Press "Power Button" of Air Fry Oven and turn the dial to select the "Air Fry" mode.
2. Press the Time button and again turn the dial to set the cooking time to 10 minutes.
3. Now push the Temp button and rotate the dial to set the temperature at 355 degrees F.
4. Press "Start/Pause" button to start.
5. When the unit beeps to show that it is preheated, open the lid.
6. Arrange the potato slices in "Air Fry Basket" and insert in the oven.
7. Meanwhile, in a bowl, add cream, eggs and flour and mix until a thick sauce forms.
8. Remove the potato slices from the basket.
9. Divide the potato slices in 4 ramekins evenly and top with the egg mixture evenly, followed by the cheese.
10. Press "Power Button" of Air Fry Oven and turn the dial to select the "Air Fry" mode.
11. Press the Time button and again turn the dial to set the cooking time to 10 minutes.

12. Now push the Temp button and rotate the dial to set the temperature at 390 degrees F.
13. Arrange the ramekins in "Air Fry Basket" and insert in the oven.
14. Press "Start/Pause" button to start.
15. Serve warm.

STUFFED OKRA

Cooking Time: 12 minutes
Serves: 2

Ingredients:
- 8 oz. large okra
- ¼ cup chickpea flour
- ¼ of onion, chopped
- 2 tablespoons coconut, grated freshly
- 1 teaspoon garam masala powder
- ½ teaspoon ground turmeric
- ½ teaspoon red chili powder
- ½ teaspoon ground cumin
- Salt, to taste

Directions:
1. With a knife, make a slit in each okra vertically without cutting in 2 halves.
2. In a bowl, mix together the flour, onion, grated coconut, and spices.
3. Stuff each okra with the mixture.
4. Press "Power Button" of Air Fry Oven and turn the dial to select the "Air Fry" mode.
5. Press the Time button and again turn the dial to set the cooking time to 12 minutes.
6. Now push the Temp button and rotate the dial to set the temperature at 390 degrees F.
7. Press "Start/Pause" button to start.
8. When the unit beeps to show that it is preheated, open the lid.
9. Arrange the stuffed okra in "Air Fry Basket" and insert in the oven.
10. Serve hot.

STUFFED BELL PEPPERS

Cooking Time: 15 minutes
Serves: 5

Ingredients:

- ½ small bell pepper, seeded and chopped
- 1 (15-oz.) can diced tomatoes with juice
- 1 (15-oz.) can red kidney beans, rinsed and drained
- 1 cup cooked rice
- 1½ teaspoons Italian seasoning
- 5 large bell peppers, tops removed and seeded
- ½ cup mozzarella cheese, shredded
- 1 tablespoon Parmesan cheese, grated

Directions:

1. In a bowl, mix together the chopped bell pepper, tomatoes with juice, beans, rice, and Italian seasoning.
2. Stuff each bell pepper with the rice mixture.
3. Press "Power Button" of Air Fry Oven and turn the dial to select the "Air Fry" mode.
4. Press the Time button and again turn the dial to set the cooking time to 15 minutes.
5. Now push the Temp button and rotate the dial to set the temperature at 360 degrees F.
6. Press "Start/Pause" button to start.
7. When the unit beeps to show that it is preheated, open the lid.
8. Arrange the bell peppers in "Air Fry Basket" and insert in the oven.
9. Meanwhile, in a bowl, mix together the mozzarella and Parmesan cheese.
10. After 12 minutes of cooking, top each bell pepper with cheese mixture.
11. Serve warm.

VEGGIE RATATOUILLE

Cooking Time: 15 minutes
Serves: 4

Ingredients:
- 1 green bell pepper, seeded and chopped
- 1 yellow bell pepper, seeded and chopped
- 1 eggplant, chopped
- 1 zucchini, chopped
- 3 tomatoes, chopped
- 2 small onions, chopped
- 2 garlic cloves, minced
- 2 tablespoons Herbs de Provence
- 1 tablespoon olive oil
- 1 tablespoon balsamic vinegar
- Salt and ground black pepper, as required

Directions:
1. In a large bowl, add the vegetables, garlic, Herbs de Provence, oil, vinegar, salt, and black pepper and toss to coat well.
2. Transfer vegetable mixture into a greased baking pan.
3. Press "Power Button" of Air Fry Oven and turn the dial to select the "Air Fry" mode.
4. Press the Time button and again turn the dial to set the cooking time to 15 minutes.
5. Now push the Temp button and rotate the dial to set the temperature at 355 degrees F.
6. Press "Start/Pause" button to start.
7. When the unit beeps to show that it is preheated, open the lid.
8. Arrange the pan over the "Wire Rack" and insert in the oven.
9. Serve hot.

GLAZED VEGGIES

Cooking Time: 20 minutes
Serves: 4

Ingredients:

- 2 oz. cherry tomatoes
- 2 large zucchini, chopped
- 2 green bell peppers, seeded and chopped
- 6 tablespoons olive oil, divided
- 2 tablespoons honey
- 1 teaspoon Dijon mustard
- 1 teaspoon dried herbs
- 1 teaspoon garlic paste
- Salt, as required

Directions:

1. In a parchment paper-lined baking pan, place the vegetables and drizzle with 3 tablespoons of oil.
2. Press "Power Button" of Air Fry Oven and turn the dial to select the "Air Fry" mode.
3. Press the Time button and again turn the dial to set the cooking time to 15 minutes.
4. Now push the Temp button and rotate the dial to set the temperature at 355 degrees F.
5. Press "Start/Pause" button to start.
6. When the unit beeps to show that it is preheated, open the lid.
7. Arrange the pan over the "Wire Rack" and insert in the oven.
8. Meanwhile, in a bowl, add the remaining oil, honey, mustard, herbs, garlic, salt, and black pepper and mix well.
9. After 15 minutes of cooking, add the honey mixture into vegetable mixture and mix well.
10. Now, set the temperature to 392 degrees F for 5 minutes.
11. Serve immediately.

PARMESAN MIXED VEGGIES

Cooking Time: 18 minutes
Serves: 5

Ingredients:
- 1 tablespoon olive oil
- 1 tablespoon garlic, minced
- 1 cup cauliflower florets
- 1 cup broccoli florets
- 1 cup zucchini, sliced
- ½ cup yellow squash, sliced
- ½ cup fresh mushrooms, sliced
- 1 small onion, sliced
- ¼ cup balsamic vinegar
- 1 teaspoon red pepper flakes
- Salt and ground black pepper, as required
- ¼ cup Parmesan cheese, grated

Directions:
1. In a large bowl, add all the ingredients except cheese and toss to coat well.
2. Press "Power Button" of Air Fry Oven and turn the dial to select the "Air Fry" mode.
3. Press the Time button and again turn the dial to set the cooking time to 18 minutes.
4. Now push the Temp button and rotate the dial to set the temperature at 400 degrees F.
5. Press "Start/Pause" button to start.
6. When the unit beeps to show that it is preheated, open the lid.
7. Arrange the vegetables in greased "Air Fry Basket" and insert in the oven.
8. After 8 minutes of cooking, flip the vegetables.
9. After 16 minutes of cooking, sprinkle the vegetables with cheese evenly.
10. Serve hot.

VEGGIE KABOBS

Cooking Time: 10 minutes
Serves: 6

Ingredients:
- ¼ cup carrots, peeled and chopped
- ¼ cup French beans
- ½ cup green peas
- 1 teaspoon ginger
- 3 garlic cloves, peeled
- 3 green chilies
- ¼ cup fresh mint leaves
- ½ cup cottage cheese
- 2 medium boiled potatoes, mashed
- ½ teaspoon five spice powder
- Salt, to taste
- 2 tablespoons corn flour
- Olive oil cooking spray

Directions:
1. In a food processor, add the carrot, beans, peas, ginger, garlic, mint, cheese and pulse until smooth.
2. Transfer the mixture into a bowl.
3. Add the potato, five spice powder, salt and corn flour and mix until well combined.
4. Divide the mixture into equal sized small balls.
5. Press each ball around a skewer in a sausage shape.
6. Spray the skewers with cooking spray.
7. Press "Power Button" of Air Fry Oven and turn the dial to select the "Air Fry" mode.
8. Press the Time button and again turn the dial to set the cooking time to 10 minutes.
9. Now push the Temp button and rotate the dial to set the temperature at 390 degrees F.
10. Press "Start/Pause" button to start.

11. When the unit beeps to show that it is preheated, open the lid.
12. Arrange the skewers in greased "Air Fry Basket" and insert in the oven.
13. Serve warm.

BEANS & VEGGIE BURGERS

Cooking Time: 22 minutes
Serves: 4

Ingredients:
- 1 cup cooked black beans
- 2 cups boiled potatoes, peeled and mashed
- 1 cup fresh spinach, chopped
- 1 cup fresh mushrooms, chopped
- 2 teaspoons Chile lime seasoning
- Olive oil cooking spray

Directions:
1. In a large bowl, add the beans, potatoes, spinach, mushrooms, and seasoning and with your hands, mix until well combined.
2. Make 4 equal-sized patties from the mixture.
3. Spray the patties with cooking spray evenly.
4. Press "Power Button" of Air Fry Oven and turn the dial to select the "Air Fry" mode.
5. Press the Time button and again turn the dial to set the cooking time to 22 minutes.
6. Now push the Temp button and rotate the dial to set the temperature at 370 degrees F.
7. Press "Start/Pause" button to start.
8. When the unit beeps to show that it is preheated, open the lid.
9. Arrange the skewers in greased "Air Fry Basket" and insert in the oven.
10. Flip the patties once after 12 minutes.

MARINATED TOFU

Cooking Time: 25 minutes
Serves: 4

Ingredients:
- 2 tablespoon low-sodium soy sauce
- 2 tablespoon fish sauce
- 1 teaspoon olive oil
- 12 oz. extra-firm tofu, drained and cubed into 1-inch size
- 1 teaspoon butter, melted

Directions:
1. In a large bowl, add the soy sauce, fish sauce and oil and mix until well combined.
2. Add the tofu cubes and toss to coat well.
3. Set aside to marinate for about 30 minutes, tossing occasionally.
4. Press "Power Button" of Air Fry Oven and turn the dial to select the "Air Fry" mode.
5. Press the Time button and again turn the dial to set the cooking time to 25 minutes.
6. Now push the Temp button and rotate the dial to set the temperature at 355 degrees F.
7. Press "Start/Pause" button to start.
8. When the unit beeps to show that it is preheated, open the lid.
9. Arrange the tofu cubes in greased "Air Fry Basket" and insert in the oven.
10. Flip the tofu after every 10 minutes during the cooking.
11. Serve hot.

CRUSTED TOFU

Cooking Time: 28 minutes
Serves: 3

Ingredients:
- 1 (14-oz.) block firm tofu, pressed and cubed into ½-inch size

- 2 tablespoons cornstarch
- ¼ cup rice flour
- Salt and ground black pepper, as required
- 2 tablespoons olive oil

Directions:

1. In a bowl, mix together the cornstarch, rice flour, salt, and black pepper.
2. Coat the tofu with flour mixture evenly.
3. Then, drizzle the tofu with oil.
4. Press "Power Button" of Air Fry Oven and turn the dial to select the "Air Fry" mode.
5. Press the Time button and again turn the dial to set the cooking time to 28 minutes.
6. Now push the Temp button and rotate the dial to set the temperature at 360 degrees F.
7. Press "Start/Pause" button to start.
8. When the unit beeps to show that it is preheated, open the lid.
9. Arrange the tofu cubes in greased "Air Fry Basket" and insert in the oven.
10. Flip the tofu cubes once halfway through.
11. Serve hot.

TOFU WITH ORANGE SAUCE

Cooking Time: 10 minutes
Serves: 4

Ingredients:

For Tofu
- 1 lb. extra-firm tofu, pressed and cubed
- 1 tablespoon cornstarch
- 1 tablespoon tamari

For Sauce
- ½ cup water
- 1/3 cup fresh orange juice
- 1 tablespoon honey

- 1 teaspoon orange zest, grated
- 1 teaspoon garlic, minced
- 1 teaspoon fresh ginger, minced
- 2 teaspoons cornstarch
- ¼ teaspoon red pepper flakes, crushed

Directions:

1. In a bowl, add the tofu, cornstarch, and tamari and toss to coat well.
2. Set the tofu aside to marinate for at least 15 minutes.
3. Press "Power Button" of Air Fry Oven and turn the dial to select the "Air Fry" mode.
4. Press the Time button and again turn the dial to set the cooking time to 10 minutes.
5. Now push the Temp button and rotate the dial to set the temperature at 390 degrees F.
6. Press "Start/Pause" button to start.
7. When the unit beeps to show that it is preheated, open the lid.
8. Arrange the tofu cubes in greased "Air Fry Basket" and insert in the oven.
9. Flip the tofu cubes once halfway through.
10. Meanwhile, for the sauce: in a small pan, add all the ingredients over medium-high heat and bring to a boil, stirring continuously.
11. Transfer the tofu into a serving bowl with the sauce and gently stir to combine.
12. Serve immediately.

TOFU WITH CAPERS

Cooking Time: 20 minutes
Serves: 4

Ingredients:

For Marinade
- ¼ cup fresh lemon juice
- 2 tablespoons fresh parsley
- 1 garlic clove, peeled
- Salt and ground black pepper, as required

For Tofu
- 1 (14-oz.) block extra-firm tofu, pressed and cut into 8 rectangular cutlets
- ½ cup mayonnaise
- 1 cup panko breadcrumbs

For Sauce
- 1 cup vegetable broth
- ¼ cup lemon juice
- 1 garlic clove, peeled
- 2 tablespoons fresh parsley
- 2 teaspoons cornstarch
- Salt and ground black pepper, as required
- 2 tablespoons capers

Directions:

1. For marinade: in a food processor, add all the ingredients and pulse until smooth.
2. In a bowl, mix together the marinade and tofu.
3. Set aside for about 15-30 minutes.
4. In 2 shallow bowls, place the mayonnaise and panko breadcrumbs respectively.
5. Coat the tofu pieces with mayonnaise and then, roll into the panko.
6. Press "Power Button" of Air Fry Oven and turn the dial to select the "Air Fry" mode.
7. Press the Time button and again turn the dial to set the cooking time to 20 minutes.
8. Now push the Temp button and rotate the dial to set the temperature at 375 degrees F.
9. Press "Start/Pause" button to start.
10. When the unit beeps to show that it is preheated, open the lid.
11. Arrange the tofu cubes in greased "Air Fry Basket" and insert in the oven.
12. Flip the tofu cubes once halfway through.
13. Meanwhile, for the sauce: add broth, lemon juice, garlic, parsley, cornstarch, salt and black pepper in a food processor and pulse until smooth.
14. Transfer the sauce into a small pan and stir in the capers.
15. Place the pan over medium heat and bring to a boil.
16. Reduce the heat to low and simmer for about 5-7 minutes, stirring continuously.
17. Transfer the tofu cubes onto serving plates.

18. Top with the sauce and serve.

TOFU IN SWEET & SOUR SAUCE

Cooking Time: 20 minutes
Serves: 4

Ingredients:

For Tofu
- 1 (14-oz.) block firm tofu, pressed and cubed
- ½ cup arrowroot flour
- ½ teaspoon sesame oil

For Sauce
- 4 tablespoons low-sodium soy sauce
- 1½ tablespoons rice vinegar
- 1½ tablespoons chili sauce
- 1 tablespoon agave nectar
- 2 large garlic cloves, minced
- 1 teaspoon fresh ginger, peeled and grated
- 2 scallions (green part), chopped

Directions:

1. In a bowl, mix together the tofu, arrowroot flour, and sesame oil.
2. Press "Power Button" of Air Fry Oven and turn the dial to select the "Air Fry" mode.
3. Press the Time button and again turn the dial to set the cooking time to 20 minutes.
4. Now push the Temp button and rotate the dial to set the temperature at 360 degrees F.
5. Press "Start/Pause" button to start.
6. When the unit beeps to show that it is preheated, open the lid.
7. Arrange the tofu cubes in greased "Air Fry Basket" and insert in the oven.
8. Flip the tofu cubes once halfway through.
9. Meanwhile, for the sauce: in a bowl, add all the ingredients except scallions and beat until well combined.

10. Transfer the tofu into a skillet with sauce over medium heat and cook for about 3 minutes, stirring occasionally.
11. Garnish with scallions and serve hot.

MAC N' CHEESE

Cooking Time: 25 minutes
Serves: 4

Ingredients:
- Cheddar cheese – 2 cups, shredded and divided
- Cornstarch – 1 tsp.
- Heavy whipping cream – 2 cups
- Dry macaroni – 2 cups

Directions:
1. In a bowl, place 1½ cups of cheese and cornstarch and mix well. Set aside. In another bowl, place the remaining cheese, whipping cream and macaroni and mix well. Transfer the macaroni mixture into a baking dish that will fit in the Vortex Air Fryer Oven. With a piece of foil, cover the baking dish that will fit in the Vortex Air Fryer Oven. Arrange the drip pan in the bottom of the Instant Vortex Air Fryer Oven cooking chamber. Select "Air Fry" and then adjust the temperature to 310 °F. Set the time for 25 minutes and press "Start". When the display shows "Add Food" insert the baking dish in the center position. When the display shows "Turn Food" do not turn food. After 15 minutes, remove the foil and top the macaroni mixture with cornstarch mixture. When cooking time is complete, remove the baking dish from the Vortex Oven. Serve warm.

SNACKS & APPETIZERS

VEGGIE PASTRIES

Cooking Time: 30 minutes
Serves: 8

Ingredients:
- Large potatoes – 2, peeled
- Olive oil – 1 tbsp.
- Carrot – ½ cup, peeled and chopped
- Onion – ½ cup, chopped
- Garlic cloves – 2, minced
- Fresh ginger – 2 tbsps. minced
- Green peas – ½ cup, shelled
- Salt and ground black pepper, as required
- Puff pastry sheets – 3

Directions:
1. In a pan of the boiling water, c0ok the potatoes for about 15-20 minutes. Drain the potatoes well and with a potato masher, mash the potatoes. In a skillet, heat oil over medium heat and sauté the carrot, onion, ginger, and garlic for about 4-5 minutes. Drain all the fat from the skillet. Stir in the mashed potatoes, peas, salt, and black pepper and cook for about 1-2 minutes. Remove the potato mixture from heat and set aside to cool completely. Arrange the puff pastry onto a smooth surface. Cut each puff pastry sheet into four pieces and then cut each piece in a round shape. Place about 2 tbsps. Of veggie filling over each pastry round. With your wet fingers, moisten the edges. Fold each pastry round in half to seal the filling. With a fork, firmly press the edges. Arrange the pastries onto a cooking tray. Arrange the drip pan in the bottom of the Instant Vortex Air Fryer Oven cooking chamber. Select "Air Fry" and then adjust the temperature to 390 °F. Set the time for 5 minutes and press "Start". When the display shows "Add Food" insert the cooking tray in the center position. When the display shows "Turn Food" turn the veggie pastries. When cooking time is complete,

remove the tray from theVortex Oven. Serve warm.

PORK SPRING ROLLS

Cooking Time: 22 minutes
Serves: 6

Ingredients:
- Pork sausage – ½ lb.
- Cheddar cheese – ½ cup, shredded
- Monterrey Jack cheese – ½ cup, shredded
- Scallion – 1 tbsp. chopped
- Large eggs – 4
- 2% milk – 1 tbsp.
- Salt and ground black pepper, as required
- Butter – 1 tbsp.
- Egg roll wrappers – 12
- Olive oil cooking spray

Directions:
1. Heat a small nonstick skillet over medium heat and cook the sausage for about 5-6 minutes, breaking into crumbles. Drain the grease from skillet. Stir in the cheeses and scallion and transfer the mixture into a bowl. In a small bowl, add the eggs, milk, salt and black pepper and beat until well combined. In another small skillet, melt the butter over medium heat. Add the egg mixture and cook for about 2-3 minutes, stirring continuously. Remove from the heat and stir with the sausage mixture. Arrange 1 egg roll wrapper onto a smooth surface. Place about ¼ a cup of filling over one corner of a wrapper, just below the center. Fold the bottom corner over the filling. With wet fingers, moisten the remaining wrapper edges. Fold side corners toward center over filling. Roll egg roll up tightly and with your fingers, press at tip to seal. Repeat with the remaining wrappers and filling. Arrange the 6 rolls onto the greased cooking tray and spray with the cooking spray. Arrange the drip pan in the bottom of the Instant Vortex Air Fryer Oven cooking chamber. Select "Air Fry" and then adjust the temperature to 400 °F. Set the time for 8 minutes and press "Start". When the display shows "Add Food" insert the cooking tray in the center position. When

the display shows "Turn Food" turn the rolls and spray with the cooking spray. Repeat with the remaining wrappers and filling. Serve warm.

POTATO BREAD ROLLS

Cooking Time: 33 minutes
Serves: 8

Ingredients:
- Large potatoes – 5, peeled
- Vegetable oil – 2 tbsps. divided
- Small onions – 2, chopped finely
- Green chilies – 2, seeded and chopped
- Curry leaves – 2
- Ground turmeric – ½ tsp.
- Salt, as required
- Bread slices – 8, trimmed

Directions:
1. In a pan of boiling water, add the potatoes and cook for about 15-20 minutes. Drain the potatoes well and with a potato masher, mash the potatoes. In a skillet, heat 1 tsp. of oil over a medium heat and sauté the onion for about 4-5 minutes. Add the green chilies, curry leaves, and turmeric and sauté for about 1 minute. Add the mashed potatoes, and salt and mix well. Remove from the heat and set aside to cool completely. Make 8 equal-sized oval-shaped patties from the mixture. Wet the bread slices completely with water. Press each bread slice between your hands to remove the excess water. Place 1 bread slice in your palm and place 1 patty in the center. Roll the bread slice in a spindle shape and seal the edges to secure the filling. Coat the roll with some oil. Repeat with the remaining slices, filling and oil. Arrange the rolls onto the greased cooking tray and spray with the cooking spray. Arrange the drip pan in the bottom of the Instant Vortex Air Fryer Oven cooking chamber. Select "Air Fry" and then adjust the temperature to 390 °F. Set the time for 13 minutes and press "Start". When the display shows "Add Food" insert the cooking tray in the center position. When the display shows "Turn Food" turn the rolls and spray with the cooking spray. Repeat with the remaining wrappers and filling. Serve warm.

CHEDDAR BISCUITS

Cooking Time: 10 minutes
Serves: 8

Ingredients:
- Unbleached all-purpose flour – 1/3 cup
- Cayenne pepper – 1/8 tsp.
- Smoked paprika – 1/8 tsp.
- Pinch of garlic powder
- Salt and ground black pepper, as required
- Sharp Cheddar cheese – ½ cup, shredded
- Butter – 2 tbsps. Softened
- Nonstick cooking spray

Directions:
1. In a food processor, add the flour, spices, salt and black pepper and pulse until well combined. Add the cheese and butter and pulse until a smooth dough forms. Place the dough onto a lightly floured surface. Make 16 small equal-sized balls from the dough and press each slightly. Arrange the biscuits onto the greased rack and spray with cooking spray. Arrange the drip pan in the bottom of the Instant Vortex Air Fryer Oven cooking chamber. Select "Bake" and then adjust the temperature to 330 °F. Set the time for 10 minutes and press "Start". When the display shows "Add Food" insert the rack in the center position. When the display shows "Turn Food" do not turn food. When cooking time is complete, remove the rack from the Vortex Oven. Place the rack aside for about 10 minutes. Carefully, invert the biscuits onto the wire rack to cool completely before serving.

CHEDDAR BISCUITS

Cooking Time: 10 minutes
Serves: 8

Ingredients:
- 1/3 cup unbleached all-purpose flour
- 1/8 teaspoon cayenne pepper
- 1/8 teaspoon smoked paprika

- Pinch of garlic powder
- Salt and ground black pepper, as required
- ½ cup sharp cheddar cheese, shredded
- 2 tablespoons butter, softened
- Nonstick cooking spray

Directions:

1. In a food processor, add the flour, spices, salt and black pepper and pulse until well combined.
2. Add the cheese and butter and pulse until a smooth dough forms.
3. Place the dough onto a lightly floured surface.
4. Make 16 small equal-sized balls from the dough and press each slightly.
5. Press "Power Button" of Air Fry Oven and turn the dial to select the "Air Bake" mode.
6. Press the Time button and again turn the dial to set the cooking time to 10 minutes.
7. Now push the Temp button and rotate the dial to set the temperature at 330 degrees F.
8. Press "Start/Pause" button to start.
9. When the unit beeps to show that it is preheated, open the lid.
10. Arrange the biscuits in greased "Air Fry Basket" and insert in the oven.
11. Place the basket onto a wire rack for about 10 minutes.
12. Carefully, invert the biscuits onto the wire rack to cool completely before serving.

LEMON BISCUITS

Cooking Time: 5 minutes
Serves: 10

Ingredients:

- 8½ oz. self-rising flour
- 3½ oz. caster sugar
- 3½ oz. cold butter
- 1 small egg
- 1 teaspoon fresh lemon zest, grated finely

- 2 tablespoons fresh lemon juice
- 1 teaspoon vanilla extract

Directions:

1. In a large bowl, mix together flour and sugar.
2. With a pastry cutter, cut cold butter and mix until a coarse crumb forms.
3. Add the egg, lemon zest and lemon juice and mix until a soft dough forms.
4. Place the dough onto a floured surface and roll the dough.
5. Cut the dough into medium-sized biscuits.
6. Arrange the biscuits into a baking pan in a single layer and coat with the butter.
7. Press "Power Button" of Air Fry Oven and turn the dial to select the "Air Fry" mode.
8. Press the Time button and again turn the dial to set the cooking time to 5 minutes.
9. Now push the Temp button and rotate the dial to set the temperature at 355 degrees F.
10. Press "Start/Pause" button to start.
11. When the unit beeps to show that it is preheated, open the lid.
12. Arrange pan over the "Wire Rack" and insert in the oven.
13. Place the baking pan onto a wire rack for about 10 minutes.
14. Carefully, invert the biscuits onto the wire rack to cool completely before serving.

POTATO BREAD ROLLS

Cooking Time: 33 minutes
Serves: 8

Ingredients:

- 5 large potatoes, peeled
- 2 tablespoons vegetable oil, divided
- 2 small onions, finely chopped
- 2 green chilies, seeded and chopped
- 2 curry leaves
- ½ teaspoon ground turmeric
- Salt, as required

- 8 bread slices, trimmed

Directions:
1. In a pan of a boiling water, add the potatoes and cook for about 15-20 minutes.
2. Drain the potatoes well and with a potato masher, mash the potatoes.
3. In a skillet, heat 1 teaspoon of oil over a medium heat and sauté the onion for about 4-5 minutes.
4. Add the green chilies, curry leaves, and turmeric and sauté for about 1 minute.
5. Add the mashed potatoes, and salt and mix well.
6. Remove from the heat and set aside to cool completely.
7. Make 8 equal-sized oval-shaped patties from the mixture.
8. Wet the bread slices completely with water.
9. Press each bread slice between your hands to remove the excess water.
10. Place 1 bread slice in your palm and place 1 patty in the center.
11. Roll the bread slice in a spindle shape and seal the edges to secure the filling.
12. Coat the roll with some oil.
13. Repeat with the remaining slices, filling and oil.
14. Press "Power Button" of Air Fry Oven and turn the dial to select the "Air Fry" mode.
15. Press the Time button and again turn the dial to set the cooking time to 13 minutes.
16. Now push the Temp button and rotate the dial to set the temperature at 390 degrees F.
17. Press "Start/Pause" button to start.
18. When the unit beeps to show that it is preheated, open the lid.
19. Arrange the bread rolls in "Air Fry Basket" and insert in the oven.
20. Serve warm.

VEGGIE SPRING ROLLS

Cooking Time: 5 minutes
Serves: 6

Ingredients:
- 1 tablespoon vegetable oil, divided
- 14 oz. fresh mushrooms, sliced

- ½ oz. canned water chestnuts, sliced
- ½ teaspoon fresh ginger, finely grated
- ½ oz. bean sprouts
- ½ of small carrot, peeled and cut into matchsticks
- 1 scallion (green part), chopped
- ½ tablespoon soy sauce
- ½ teaspoon Chinese five-spice powder
- 1½ oz. cooked shrimps
- 6 spring roll wrappers
- 1 small egg, beaten

Directions:

1. In a skillet, heat 1 tablespoon of oil over medium heat and sauté the mushrooms, water chestnuts, and ginger for about 2-3 minutes.
2. Add the beans sprouts, carrot, scallion, soy sauce, and five-spice powder and sauté for about 1 minute.
3. Stir in the shrimps and remove from heat. Set aside to cool.
4. Arrange the spring rolls onto a smooth surface.
5. Divide the veggie mixture evenly between spring rolls.
6. Roll the wrappers around the filling and seal with beaten egg.
7. Coat each roll with the remaining oil.
8. Repeat with the remaining slices, filling and oil.
9. Press "Power Button" of Air Fry Oven and turn the dial to select the "Air Fry" mode.
10. Press the Time button and again turn the dial to set the cooking time to 5 minutes.
11. Now push the Temp button and rotate the dial to set the temperature at 390 degrees F.
12. Press "Start/Pause" button to start.
13. When the unit beeps to show that it is preheated, open the lid.
14. Arrange the rolls in "Air Fry Basket" and insert in the oven.
15. Serve warm.

SPINACH ROLLS

Cooking Time: 4 minutes

Serves: 6

Ingredients:
- 1 red onion, chopped
- 1 cup fresh parsley, chopped
- 1 cup fresh mint leaves, chopped
- 1 egg
- 1 cup feta cheese, crumbled
- ½ cup Romano cheese, grated
- ¼ teaspoon ground cardamom
- Salt and freshly ground black pepper, as needed
- 1 package frozen phyllo dough, thawed
- 1 (16-oz.) package frozen spinach, thawed
- 2 tablespoons olive oil

Directions:
1. In a food processor, add all the ingredients except phyllo dough and oil and pulse until smooth.
2. Place one phyllo sheet on the cutting board and cut into three rectangular strips.
3. Brush each strip with the oil.
4. Place about 1 teaspoon of spinach mixture along with the short side of a strip.
5. Roll the dough to secure the filling.
6. Repeat with the remaining phyllo sheets and spinach mixture.
7. Press "Power Button" of Air Fry Oven and turn the dial to select the "Air Fry" mode.
8. Press the Time button and again turn the dial to set the cooking time to 4 minutes.
9. Now push the Temp button and rotate the dial to set the temperature at 355 degrees F.
10. Press "Start/Pause" button to start.
11. When the unit beeps to show that it is preheated, open the lid.
12. Arrange the rolls in "Air Fry Basket" and insert in the oven.
13. Serve warm.

CHEESE PASTRIES

Cooking Time: 10 minutes
Serves: 6

Ingredients:
- 1 egg yolk
- 4 oz. feta cheese, crumbled
- 1 scallion, finely chopped
- 2 tablespoons fresh parsley, finely chopped
- Salt and ground black pepper, as needed
- 2 frozen phyllo pastry sheets, thawed
- 2 tablespoons olive oil

Directions:
1. In a large bowl, add the egg yolk, and beat well.
2. Add the feta cheese, scallion, parsley, salt, and black pepper and mix well.
3. Cut each pastry sheet in three strips.
4. Add about 1 teaspoon of feta mixture on the underside of a strip.
5. Fold the tip of sheet over the filling in a zigzag manner to form a triangle.
6. Repeat with the remaining strips and fillings.
7. Coat each pastry with oil evenly.
8. Press "Power Button" of Air Fry Oven and turn the dial to select the "Air Fry" mode.
9. Press the Time button and again turn the dial to set the cooking time to 3 minutes.
10. Now push the Temp button and rotate the dial to set the temperature at 390 degrees F.
11. Press "Start/Pause" button to start.
12. When the unit beeps to show that it is preheated, open the lid.
13. Arrange the pastries in "Air Fry Basket" and insert in the oven.
14. After 3 minutes, set the temperature at 390 degrees F for 2 minutes.
15. Repeat with remaining pastries.
16. Serve warm.

VEGGIE PASTRIES CHILI DIP ONION DIP

Cooking Time: 45 minutes
Serves: 10

Ingredients:
- 2/3 cup onion, chopped
- 1 cup cheddar jack cheese, shredded
- ½ cup Swiss cheese, shredded
- ¼ cup Parmesan cheese, shredded
- 2/3 cup whipped salad dressing
- ½ cup milk
- Salt, as required

Directions:
1. In a large bowl, add all the ingredients and mix well.
2. Transfer the mixture into a baking pan and spread in an even layer.
3. Press "Power Button" of Air Fry Oven and turn the dial to select the "Air Bake" mode.
4. Press the Time button and again turn the dial to set the cooking time to 45 minutes.
5. Now push the Temp button and rotate the dial to set the temperature at 375 degrees F.
6. Press "Start/Pause" button to start.
7. When the unit beeps to show that it is preheated, open the lid.
8. Arrange pan over the "Wire Rack" and insert in the oven.
9. Serve hot.

FISH AND SEAFOOD RECIPES

SCALLOPS WITH SPINACH

Cooking Time: 10 minutes
Serves: 2

Ingredients:
- Heavy whipping cream – ¾ cup
- Tomato paste – 1 tbsp.
- Garlic – 1 tsp. minced
- Fresh basil – 1 tbsp. chopped
- Salt and ground black pepper, as required
- Jumbo sea scallops – 8
- Olive oil cooking spray
- Frozen spinach – 1 (12-oz.) package, thawed and drained

Directions:
1. In a bowl, place the cream, tomato paste, garlic, basil, salt, and black pepper and mix well. Spray each scallop with cooking spray evenly and then, sprinkle with a little salt and black pepper. Place the spinach in the bottom of a baking dish that will fit in the Vortex Air Fryer Oven. Arrange scallops on top of the spinach in a single layer and top with the cream mixture evenly. Arrange the drip pan in the bottom of the Instant Vortex Air Fryer Oven cooking chamber. Select "Air Fry" and then adjust the temperature to 350 °F. Set the timer for 10 minutes and press "Start". When the display shows "Add Food" insert the baking dish in the center position. When the display shows "Turn Food" do not turn food. When cooking time is complete, remove the baking dish from the Vortex Oven. Serve hot.

BARRAMUNDI FILLES WITH LEMON-BUTTER SAUCE

Cooking Time: 25 minutes
Serves: 3

Ingredients:

- 3 (½ lb) barramundi fillets
- 2 lemons, juiced
- Salt and black pepper to taste
- 6 oz butter
- ¾ cup thickened cream
- ½ cup white wine
- 2 bay leaves
- 15 black peppercorns
- 2 cloves garlic, minced
- 2 shallots, chopped

Directions

1. Preheat the Air Fryer to 390 F. Place the barramundi fillets on a baking paper and put them in the fryer basket. Cook for 15 minutes. Remove to a serving platter without the paper.
2. Place a small pan over low heat on a stove top. Add the garlic and shallots, and dry fry for 20 seconds. Add the wine, bay leaves, and peppercorns. Stir and allow the liquid to reduce by three quarters, and add the cream. Stir and let the sauce thicken into a dark cream color.
3. Add the butter, whisk it into the cream until it has fully melted. Add the lemon juice, pepper, and salt. Turn the heat off. Strain the sauce into a serving bowl. Pour the sauce over the fish and serve with a side of rice.

GARLIC-CHILI PRAWNS

Cooking Time: 12 minutes
Serves: 8

Ingredients:

- 8 prawns, cleaned
- Salt and black pepper
- ½ tsp ground cayenne
- ½ tsp chili flakes
- ½ tsp ground cumin
- ½ tsp garlic powder

Directions

1. In a bowl, season the prawns with salt and black pepper. Sprinkle cayenne, flakes, cumin and garlic and stir to coat. Spray the air fryer's basket with oil and arrange the prawns in an even layer. Cook for 8 minutes at 340 F, turning once halfway through. Serve with fresh lettuce leaves or sweet chili/mayo sauce.

CATFISH FILLETS WITH PARSLEY

Cooking Time: 40 minutes
Serves: 2

Ingredients:
- 2 catfish fillets
- 3 tbsp breadcrumbs
- 1 tsp cayenne pepper
- 1 tsp dry fish seasoning, of choice
- 2 sprigs parsley, chopped
- Salt to taste, optional

Directions

1. Preheat Air Fryer to 400 F. Meanwhile, pour all the dry ingredients, except the parsley, in a zipper bag. Pat dry and add the fish pieces. Close the bag and shake to coat the fish well. Do this with one fish piece at a time.
2. Lightly spray the fish with olive oil. Arrange them in the fryer basket, one at a time depending on the size of the fish. Close the Air Fryer and cook for 10 minutes. Flip the fish and cook further for 10 minutes. For extra crispiness, cook for 3 more minutes. Garnish with parsley and serve as a lunch accompaniment.

GARLIC SALMON WITH SOY SAUCE

Cooking Time: 13 minutes
Serves: 1

Ingredients:
- 1 salmon fillet

- 1 tbsp soy sauce
- ¼ tsp garlic powder
- Salt and black pepper to taste

Directions

1. Preheat the Air fryer to 350 F, and combine soy sauce with garlic powder, salt and pepper. Brush the mixture over salmon. Place the salmon onto a sheet of parchment paper and into the air fryer; cook for 10 minutes.

CREAMY CRAB CROQUETTES

Cooking Time: 30 minutes
Serves: 4

Ingredients:

Filling:
- 1 ½ lb lump crab meat
- 3 egg whites, beaten
- ⅓ cup sour cream
- ⅓ cup mayonnaise
- 1 ½ tbsp olive oil
- 1 red pepper, chopped finely
- ⅓ cup chopped red onion
- 2 ½ tbsp chopped celery
- ½ tsp chopped tarragon
- ½ tsp chopped chives
- 1 tsp chopped parsley
- 1 tsp cayenne pepper

Breading:
- 1 ½ cup breadcrumbs
- 2 tsp olive oil
- 1 cup flour
- 4 eggs, beaten
- Salt to taste

Directions

1. Place a skillet over medium heat on a stove top, add 1 ½ tbsp olive oil, red pepper, onion, and celery. Sauté for 5 minutes or until sweaty and translucent. Turn off heat. Add the breadcrumbs, the remaining olive oil, and salt to a food processor. Blend to mix evenly; set aside. In 2 separate bowls, add the flour and 4 eggs respectively; set aside.

2. In a separate bowl, add the crabmeat, mayo, egg whites, sour cream, tarragon, chives, parsley, cayenne pepper, and the celery sauté and mix evenly. Form bite-size balls from the mixture and place into a plate.

3. Preheat the Air Fryer to 390 F. Dip each crab meatball (croquettes) in the eggs mixture and press them in the breadcrumb mixture. Place the croquettes in the fryer basket, 12 to 15 at a time; avoid overcrowding.

4. Close the Air Fryer and cook for 10 minutes or until golden brown. Remove them and plate them. Serve the crab croquettes with tomato dipping sauce and a side of vegetable fries.

BABY OCTOPUS WITH CAPERS AND FENNEL SALAD

Cooking Time: 50 minutes
Serves: 3

Ingredients:

- 1 lb baby octopus, thoroughly cleaned
- 1 ½ tbsp olive oil
- 2 cloves garlic, minced
- 1 ½ tbsp capers
- 1 ¼ tbsp balsamic glaze
- 1 bunch parsley, chopped roughly
- 1 bunch baby fennel, chopped
- 1 cup semi-dried tomatoes, chopped
- 1 red onion, sliced
- A handful of arugula
- Salt and black pepper to taste
- ¼ cup chopped grilled Halloumi
- 1 long red chili, minced
- 1 ½ cups water

Directions

1. Pour the water in a pot and bring to boil over medium heat on a stove top. Cut the octopus into bite sizes and add it to the boiling water for 45 seconds; drain the water. Add the garlic, olive oil, and octopus in a bowl. Coat the octopus with the garlic and olive oil. Leave to marinate for 20 minutes.

2. Preheat the Air Fryer to 390 F. Place the octopus in the fryer basket and grill for 5 minutes. Meanwhile, in a salad mixing bowl, add the capers, halloumi, chili, tomatoes, olives, parsley, red onion, fennel, octopus, arugula, and balsamic glaze. Season with salt and pepper and mix. Serve with a side of toasts.

RICH SEAFOOD PIE

Cooking Time: 60 minutes
Serves: 3

Ingredients:

- 1 cup seafood marinara mix
- 1 lb russet potatoes, peeled and quartered
- 1 cup water
- 1 carrot, grated
- ½ head baby fennel, grated
- 1 bunch dill sprigs, chopped
- 1 sprig parsley, chopped
- A handful of baby spinach
- 1 small tomato, diced
- ½ celery sticks, grated
- 2 tbsp butter
- 1 tbsp milk
- ½ cup grated Cheddar cheese
- 1 small red chili, minced
- ½ lemon, juiced
- Salt and black pepper to taste

Directions

1. Add the potatoes to a pan, pour the water, and bring to a boil over medium heat on a stove top. Use a fork to check that if they are soft and mash-able, after about

12 minutes. Drain the water and use a potato masher to mash. Add the butter, milk, salt, and pepper. Mash until smooth and well mixed; set aside.

2. In a bowl, add the celery, carrots, cheese, chili, fennel, parsley, lemon juice, seafood mix, dill, tomato, spinach, salt, and pepper; mix well.

3. Preheat the Air Fryer to 330 F. In a 6 inches casserole dish, add half of the carrots mixture and level. Top with half of the potato mixture and level. Place the dish in the Air Fryer and bake for 20 minutes until golden brown and the seafood is properly cooked. Remove the dish and add the remaining seafood mixture and level out.

4. Top with the remaining potato mash and level it too. Place the dish back to the fryer and cook at 330 F for 20 minutes. Once ready, ensure that it's well cooked, and remove the dish. Slice the pie and serve with a green salad.

SAVORY SALMON WITH VEGETABLES

Cooking Time: 25 minutes
Serves: 2

Ingredients:
- 2-3 fingerling potatoes, thinly sliced
- ½ bulb fennel, thinly sliced
- 4 tbsp melted butter
- Salt and black pepper to taste
- 1-2 tsp fresh dill
- 2 sockeye salmon fillets (6 oz each)
- 8 cherry tomatoes, halved
- ¼ cup fish stock

Directions
1. Preheat Air Fryer to 400 F, and boil salted water in a small saucepan over medium heat. Add the potatoes and blanch for 2 minutes; drain the potatoes. Cut 2 large-sized rectangles of parchment paper of 13x15 inch size.
2. In a large bowl, mix potatoes, melted butter, fennel, fresh ground pepper, and salt. Divide the mixture between parchment paper pieces and sprinkle dill on top. Place fillet on top of veggie piles; season with salt and pepper.
3. Add cherry tomato on top of each veggie pile and drizzle butter; pour fish stock

on top. Fold the squares and seal them. Preheat your air fryer to 400 F, and cook the packets for 10 minutes. Garnish with a bit of dill and enjoy!

MOZZARELLA & SMOKED FISH TART

Cooking Time: 35 minutes
Serves: 5

Ingredients:
- 1 quiche pastry case
- 5 eggs, lightly beaten
- 4 tbsp heavy cream
- ¼ cup finely chopped green onions
- ¼ cup chopped parsley
- 1 tsp baking powder
- Salt and black pepper
- 1 lb smoked fish
- 1 cup shredded mozzarella cheese

Directions
1. In a bowl, whisk eggs, cream, scallions, parsley, baking powder, salt and black. Add in fish and cheese, stir to combine. Line the air fryer with baking paper. Pour the mixture into the pastry case and place it gently inside the air fryer. Cook for 25 minutes at 360 F. Check past 15 minutes, so it's not overcooked.

HOMEMADE CRISPY FISH FINGERS

Cooking Time: 20 minutes
Serves: 8

Ingredients:
- 2 fresh white fish fillets, cut into 4 fingers each
- 1 egg, beaten
- ½ cup buttermilk
- 1 cup panko breadcrumbs

- Salt and black pepper

Directions

1. In a bowl, mix egg and buttermilk. On a plate, mix and spread crumbs, salt, and black pepper. Dip each finger into the egg mixture, then roll it up in the crumbs, and spray with olive oil. Arrange them in the air fryer and cook for 10 minutes at 340 F, turning once halfway through. Serve with garlic mayo and lemon wedges.

SHRIMP SKEWERS WITH PINEAPPLE

Prep Time: 10 minutes
Cooking Time: 6 minutes
Serves: 4

Ingredients:

- 1/2 cup coconut milk
- 4 teaspoons Tabasco Sauce
- 2 teaspoons soy sauce
- 1/4 cup orange juice
- 1/4 cup lime juice
- 1 lb.   shrimp, peeled and deveined
- 3/4 lb. pineapple chunks, diced

Directions:

1. Toss the shrimp and pineapple with all other ingredients in a bowl.
2. Thread shrimp and pineapple on the skewers.
3. Place the shrimp pineapple skewers in the Air fryer Basket.
4. Press "Power Button" of Air Fry Oven and turn the dial to select the "Air fry" mode.
5. Press the Time button and again turn the dial to set the cooking time to 6 minutes.
6. Now push the Temp button and rotate the dial to set the temperature at 350 degrees F.
7. Once preheated, place the Air fryer basket in the oven and close its lid.
8. Toss and flip the shrimp when cooked halfway through.
9. Serve warm.

TERIYAKI SHRIMP SKEWER

Cooking Time: 6 minutes
Serves: 4

Ingredients:

Shrimp Skewers:
- 1 lb. shrimp, peeled and deveined
- 1 pineapple, peeled, and cut into chunks
- 2 zucchinis, cut into thick slices
- 3 red and orange bell peppers, cut into 2-inch chunks
- Bamboo or metal skewers

Teriyaki BBQ Sauce:
- 1/2 cup teriyaki sauce
- 2 tablespoon fish sauce
- 2 tablespoon chili garlic sauce

Directions:
1. Toss the shrimp and veggies with all other ingredients in a bowl.
2. Thread shrimp and veggies on the skewers alternately.
3. Place the shrimp vegetable skewers in the Air fryer Basket.
4. Mix the teriyaki sauce ingredients in a bowl and pour over the skewers.
5. Press "Power Button" of Air Fry Oven and turn the dial to select the "Air fry" mode.
6. Press the Time button and again turn the dial to set the cooking time to 6 minutes.
7. Now push the Temp button and rotate the dial to set the temperature at 350 degrees F.
8. Once preheated, place the Air fryer basket in the oven and close its lid.
9. Toss and flip the shrimp when cooked halfway through.
10. Serve warm.

CAJUN SHRIMP SKEWERS PRAWN BURGERS

Cooking Time: 6 minutes

Serves: 2

Ingredients:
- ½ cup prawns, peeled, deveined and chopped very finely
- ½ cup breadcrumbs
- 2-3 tablespoons onion, chopped finely
- ½ teaspoon ginger, minced
- ½ teaspoon garlic, minced
- ½ teaspoon red chili powder
- ½ teaspoon ground cumin
- ¼ teaspoon ground turmeric
- Salt and ground black pepper, as required

Directions:
1. In a bowl, add all ingredients and mix until well combined.
2. Make small sized patties from mixture.
3. Press "Power Button" of Air Fry Oven and turn the dial to select the "Air Fry" mode.
4. Press the Time button and again turn the dial to set the cooking time to 6 minutes.
5. Now push the Temp button and rotate the dial to set the temperature at 355 degrees F.
6. Press "Start/Pause" button to start.
7. When the unit beeps to show that it is preheated, open the lid.
8. Arrange the patties in greased "Air Fry Basket" and insert in the oven.
9. Serve hot.

POULTRY RECIPES

CAYENNE CHICKEN WITH COCONUT FLAKES

Cooking Time: 25 minutes
Serves: 4

Ingredients:
- 3 chicken breasts, cubed
- Oil as needed
- 3 cups coconut flakes
- 3 whole eggs, beaten
- ½ cup cornstarch
- Salt to taste
- 1 tbsp cayenne pepper
- Pepper to taste

Directions
1. Preheat your Air Fryer to 350 F. In a bowl, mix salt, cornstarch, cayenne pepper, pepper. In another bowl, add beaten eggs and coconut flakes. Cover chicken with pepper mix. Dredge chicken in the egg mix. Cover chicken with oil. Place the prepared chicken in your Air Fryer's cooking basket and cook for 20 minutes.

HONEY CHICKEN WINGS

Cooking Time: 25 minutes
Serves: 4

Ingredients:
- 8 chicken drumsticks
- 1 tbsp olive oil
- 1 tbsp sesame oil
- 4 tbsp honey
- 3 tbsp light soy sauce

- 2 crushed garlic clove
- 1 small knob fresh ginger, grated
- 1 small bunch coriander, chopped
- 2 tbsp sesame seeds, toasted

Directions

1. Add all ingredients in a freezer bag, except sesame and coriander. Seal up and massage until the drumsticks are coated well. Preheat your Air Fryer to 400 F. Place the drumsticks in the cooking basket and cook for 10 minutes. Lower the temperature to 325 F and cook for 10 more minutes. Sprinkle with some sesame and coriander seeds.

GINGER CHICKEN WINGS

Cooking Time: 25 minutes
Serves: 3

Ingredients:
- 1 pound chicken wings
- 1 tbsp cilantro
- Salt and black pepper to taste
- 1 tbsp cashews cream
- 1 garlic clove, minced
- 1 tbsp yogurt
- 2 tbsp honey
- ½ tbsp vinegar
- ½ tbsp ginger, minced
- ½ tbsp garlic chili sauce

Directions

1. Preheat the air fryer to 360 F. Season the wings with salt and pepper, and place them in the Air Fryer, and cook for 15 minutes. In a bowl, mix the remaining ingredients. Top the chicken with sauce and cook for 5 more minutes.

ENCHILADA CHEESE CHICKEN

Cooking Time: 65 minutes
Serves: 6

Ingredients:
- 3 cups chicken breast, chopped
- 2 cups cheese, grated
- ½ cup salsa
- 1 can green chilies, chopped
- 12 flour tortillas
- 2 cans enchilada sauce

Directions
1. Preheat your Fryer to 400 F. In a bowl, mix salsa and enchilada sauce. Toss in the chopped chicken to coat. Place the chicken on the tortillas and roll; top with cheese. Place the prepared tortillas in the Air Fryer cooking basket and cook for 60 minutes. Serve with guacamole and Mexican dips!

BASIL MOZZARELLA CHICKEN

Cooking Time: 25 minutes
Serves: 6

Ingredients:
- 6 chicken breasts, cubed
- 6 basil leaves
- ¼ cup balsamic vinegar
- 6 slices tomato
- 1 tbsp butter
- 6 slices mozzarella cheese

Directions
1. Preheat your Fryer to 400 F and heat butter and balsamic vinegar in a frying pan over medium heat. Cover the chicken meat with the marinade. Place the chicken in the cooking basket and cook for 20 minutes. Cover the chicken with basil, tomato slices and cheese. Serve and enjoy!

PARMESAN CHICKEN CUTLETS

Cooking Time: 20 minutes
Serves: 4

Ingredients:
- ¼ cup Parmesan cheese, grated
- 4 chicken cutlets
- ⅛ tbsp paprika
- ¼ tsp pepper
- 2 tbsp panko breadcrumbs
- 1 tbsp parsley
- ½ tbsp garlic powder
- 2 large eggs, beaten

Directions
1. Preheat your Air Fryer to 400 F. In a bowl, mix Parmesan cheese, breadcrumbs, garlic powder, pepper, paprika and mash the mixture. Add eggs in a bowl. Dip the chicken cutlets in eggs, dredge them in cheese and panko mixture. Place the prepared cutlets in the cooking basket and cook for 15 minutes.

BUTTERMILK MARINATED CHICKEN

Cooking Time: 25 minutes
Serves: 6

Ingredients:
- 3-lb. whole chicken
- 1 tablespoon salt
- 1-pint buttermilk

Directions:
1. Place the whole chicken in a large bowl and drizzle salt on top.
2. Pour the buttermilk over it and leave the chicken soaked overnight.
3. Cover the chicken bowl and refrigerate overnight.
4. Remove the chicken from the marinade and fix it on the rotisserie rod in the Air

fryer oven.

5. Turn the dial to select the "Air Roast" mode.
6. Hit the Time button and again use the dial to set the cooking time to 25 minutes.
7. Now push the Temp button and rotate the dial to set the temperature at 370 degrees F.
8. Close its lid and allow the chicken to roast.
9. Serve warm.

THYME TURKEY BREAST

Cooking Time: 40 minutes
Serves: 4

Ingredients:
- 2 lb. turkey breast
- Salt, to taste
- Black pepper, to taste
- 4 tablespoon butter, melted
- 3 cloves garlic, minced
- 1 teaspoon thyme, chopped
- 1 teaspoon rosemary, chopped

Directions:
1. Mix butter with salt, black pepper, garlic, thyme, and rosemary in a bowl.
2. Rub this seasoning over the turkey breast liberally and place in the Air Fryer basket.
3. Turn the dial to select the "Air Fry" mode.
4. Hit the Time button and again use the dial to set the cooking time to 40 minutes.
5. Now push the Temp button and rotate the dial to set the temperature at 375 degrees F.
6. Once preheated, place the Air fryer basket inside the oven.
7. Slice and serve fresh.

ROASTED DUCK

Cooking Time: 3 hours
Serves: 12

Ingredients:

- 6 lb. whole Pekin duck
- salt
- 5 garlic cloves chopped
- 1 lemon, chopped

Glaze

- 1/2 cup balsamic vinegar
- 1 lemon, juiced
- 1/4 cup honey

Directions:

1. Place the Pekin duck in a baking tray and add garlic, lemon, and salt on top.
2. Whisk honey, vinegar, and honey in a bowl.
3. Brush this glaze over the duck liberally. Marinate overnight in the refrigerator.
4. Remove the duck from the marinade and fix it on the rotisserie rod in the Air fryer oven.
5. Turn the dial to select the "Air Roast" mode.
6. Hit the Time button and again use the dial to set the cooking time to 3 hours.
7. Now push the Temp button and rotate the dial to set the temperature at 350 degrees F.
8. Close its lid and allow the duck to roast.
9. Serve warm.

CHICKEN DRUMSTICKS

Cooking Time: 20 minutes
Serves: 8

Ingredients:

- 8 chicken drumsticks
- 2 tablespoon olive oil

- 1 teaspoon salt
- 1 teaspoon pepper
- 1 teaspoon garlic powder
- 1 teaspoon paprika
- 1/2 teaspoon cumin

Directions:

1. Mix olive oil with salt, black pepper, garlic powder, paprika, and cumin in a bowl.
2. Rub this mixture liberally over all the drumsticks.
3. Place these drumsticks in the Air fryer basket.
4. Turn the dial to select the "Air Fry" mode.
5. Hit the Time button and again use the dial to set the cooking time to 20 minutes.
6. Now push the Temp button and rotate the dial to set the temperature at 375 degrees F.
7. Once preheated, place the Air fryer basket inside the oven.
8. Flip the drumsticks when cooked halfway through.
9. Resume air frying for another rest of the 10 minutes.
10. Serve warm.

BLACKENED CHICKEN BAKE

Cooking Time: 18 minutes
Serves: 4

Ingredients:

- 4 chicken breasts
- 2 teaspoon olive oil

Seasoning:
- 1 1/2 tablespoon brown sugar
- 1 teaspoon paprika
- 1 teaspoon dried oregano
- 1/4 teaspoon garlic powder
- 1/2 teaspoon salt and pepper

Garnish:

- Chopped parsley

Directions:
1. Mix olive oil with brown sugar, paprika, oregano, garlic powder, salt, and black pepper in a bowl.
2. Place the chicken breasts in the baking tray of the Ninja Oven.
3. Pour and rub this mixture liberally over all the chicken breasts.
4. Turn the dial to select the "Bake" mode.
5. Hit the Time button and again use the dial to set the cooking time to 18 minutes.
6. Now push the Temp button and rotate the dial to set the temperature at 425 degrees F.
7. Once preheated, place the baking tray inside the oven.
8. Serve warm.

CRUSTED CHICKEN DRUMSTICKS

Cooking Time: 10 minutes
Serves: 4

Ingredients:
- 1 lb. chicken drumsticks
- 1/2 cup buttermilk
- 1/2 cup panko breadcrumbs
- 1/2 cup flour
- 1/4 teaspoon baking powder

Spice Mixture
- 1/2 teaspoon salt
- 1/2 teaspoon celery salt
- 1/4 teaspoon oregano
- 1/4 teaspoon cayenne
- 1 teaspoon paprika
- 1/4 teaspoon garlic powder
- 1/4 teaspoon dried thyme
- 1/2 teaspoon ground ginger
- 1/2 teaspoon white pepper

- 1/2 teaspoon black pepper
- 3 tablespoon butter melted

Directions:
1. Soak chicken in the buttermilk and cover to marinate overnight in the refrigerator.
2. Mix spices with flour, breadcrumbs, and baking powder in a shallow tray.
3. Remove the chicken from the milk and coat them well with the flour spice mixture
4. Place the chicken drumsticks in the Air fryer basket of the Ninja Oven.
5. Pour the melted butter over the drumsticks
6. Turn the dial to select the "Air fry" mode.
7. Hit the Time button and again use the dial to set the cooking time to 10 minutes.
8. Now push the Temp button and rotate the dial to set the temperature at 425 degrees F.
9. Once preheated, place the baking tray inside the oven.
10. Flip the drumsticks and resume cooking for another 10 minutes.
11. Serve warm.

ROASTED TURKEY BREAST

Cooking Time: 50 minutes
Serves: 6

Ingredients:
- 3 lb. boneless turkey breast
- ¼ cup mayonnaise
- 2 teaspoon poultry seasoning
- 1 teaspoon salt
- ½ teaspoon garlic powder
- ¼ teaspoon black pepper

Directions:
1. Whisk all the ingredients, including turkey in a bowl, and coat it well.
2. Place the boneless turkey breast in the Air fryer basket.
3. Rotate the dial to select the "Air fry" mode.

4. Press the Time button and again use the dial to set the cooking time to 50 minutes.
5. Now press the Temp button and rotate the dial to set the temperature at 350 degrees F.
6. Once preheated, place the air fryer basket in the Ninja oven and Close its lid to bake.
7. Slice and serve.

BRINE SOAKED TURKEY

Cooking Time: 45 minutes
Serves: 8

Ingredients:
- 7 lb. bone-in, skin-on turkey breast

Brine:
- 1/2 cup salt
- 1 lemon
- 1/2 onion
- 3 cloves garlic, smashed
- 5 sprigs fresh thyme
- 3 bay leaves
- black pepper

Turkey Breast:
- 4 tablespoon butter, softened
- 1/2 teaspoon black pepper
- 1/2 teaspoon garlic powder
- 1/4 teaspoon dried thyme
- 1/4 teaspoon dried oregano

Directions:
1. Mix the turkey brine ingredients in a pot and soak the turkey in the brine overnight.
2. Next day, remove the soaked turkey from the brine.
3. Whisk the butter, black pepper, garlic powder, oregano, and thyme.

4. Brush the butter mixture over the turkey then place it in a baking tray.
5. Press "Power Button" of Air Fry Oven and turn the dial to select the "Air Roast" mode.
6. Press the Time button and again turn the dial to set the cooking time to 45 minutes.
7. Now push the Temp button and rotate the dial to set the temperature at 370 degrees F.
8. Once preheated, place the turkey baking tray in the oven and close its lid.
9. Slice and serve warm.

MEAT RECIPES

DELICIOUS HOT STEAKS

Cooking Time: 15 minutes
Serves: 2

Ingredients:
- 2 steaks, 1-inch thick
- ½ tsp black pepper
- ½ tsp cayenne pepper
- 1 tbsp olive oil
- ½ tsp ground paprika
- Salt and black pepper to taste

Directions
1. Preheat the air fryer to 390 F. Mix olive oil, black pepper, cayenne, paprika, salt and pepper and rub onto steaks. Spread evenly. Put the steaks in the fryer, and cook for 6 minutes, turning them halfway through.

HERBY-TOMATO MEATLOAF

Cooking Time: 30 minutes
Serves: 4

Ingredients:
- 1 lb ground beef
- 2 eggs, lightly beaten
- ½ cup breadcrumbs
- 2 garlic cloves, crushed
- 1 onion, finely chopped
- 2 tbsp tomato puree
- 1 tsp mixed dried herbs

Directions

1. Line a loaf pan that fits in your fryer with baking paper. In a bowl, mix beef, eggs, breadcrumbs, garlic, onion, puree, and herbs. Gently press the mixture into the pan and slide in the air fryer. Cook for 25 minutes on 380 F. If undercooked, and slightly moist, cook for 5 more minutes. Wait 15 minutes before slicing it.

PORK RIBS WITH BBQ SAUCE

Cooking Time: 4 h 35 minutes
Serves: 2

Ingredients:

- 1 lb pork ribs
- ½ tsp five spice powder
- 1 tsp salt
- 3 garlic cloves, chopped
- 1 tsp black pepper
- 1 tsp sesame oil
- 1 tbsp honey, plus some more for brushing
- 4 tbsp barbecue sauce
- 1 tsp soy sauce

Directions:

1. Chop the ribs into smaller pieces and place them in a large bowl. In a smaller bowl, whisk together all of the other ingredients.
2. Add them to the bowl with the pork, and mix until the pork is fully coated. Cover the bowl, place it in the fridge, and let it marinate for about 4 hours. Preheat the Air fryer to 350 F and cook the ribs in Air fryer for 15 minutes.
3. Brush the ribs with some honey and cook for another 15 minutes.

CREAMY BEEF LIVER CAKES

Cooking Time: 25 minutes
Serves: 2

Ingredients:

- 1 lb beef liver, sliced
- 2 large eggs
- 1 tbsp butter
- ½ tbsp black truffle oil
- 1 tbsp cream
- Salt and black pepper

Directions

1. Preheat the Air Fryer to 320 F. Cut the liver into thin slices and refrigerate for 10 minutes. Separate the whites from the yolks and put each yolk in a cup. In another bowl, add the cream, truffle oil, salt and pepper and mix with a fork. Arrange half of the mixture in a small ramekin.
2. Pour the white of the egg and divide it equally between ramekins. Top with the egg yolks. Surround each yolk with a liver. Cook for 15 minutes and serve cool.

HOMEMADE BEEF EMPANADAS

Cooking Time: 25 minutes
Serves: 4

Ingredients:

- 1 lb ground beef
- ½ onion, diced
- 1 garlic clove, minced
- ¼ cup tomato salsa
- 4 empanada shells
- 1 egg yolk
- 2 tsp milk
- ½ tsp cumin
- Salt and black pepper to taste
- ½ tbsp olive oil

Directions

1. Grease with olive oil and set to 350 F. Meanwhile, combine the beef, onion, cumin, and garlic, in a bowl. Season with some salt and pepper. Place the beef in

the air fryer and cook for 7 minutes, flipping once halfway through.

2. Stir in the tomato salsa and set aside. In a small bowl, combine the milk and yolk. Place the empanada shells on a dry and clean surface. Divide the beef mixture between the shells. Fold the shells and seal the ends with a fork. Brush with the egg wash. Place on a lined baking sheet and bake at 350 F for 10 minutes. Serve with a cheese dip.

GROUND PORK & APPLE BURGERS

Cooking Time: 25 minutes
Serves: 2

Ingredients:
- 12 oz ground pork
- 1 apple, peeled and grated
- 1 cup breadcrumbs
- 2 eggs, beaten
- ½ tsp ground cumin
- ½ tsp ground cinnamon
- Salt and black pepper to taste

Directions
1. In a bowl, add pork, apple, breadcrumbs, cumin, eggs, cinnamon, salt, and black pepper; mix with hands. Shape into 4 even-sized burger patties. Grease the fryer with oil, arrange the patties inside the basket and cook for 14 minutes at 340 F, turning once halfway through.

CHILI ROASTED BEEF

Cooking Time: 4 hrs 20 minutes
Serves: 2

Ingredients:
- 1 lb ground beef
- ½ tsp salt

- 2 tbsp soy sauce
- ½ tsp pepper
- Thumb-sized piece of ginger, chopped
- 3 chilies, deseeded and chopped
- 4 garlic cloves, chopped
- 1 tsp brown sugar
- Juice of 1 lime
- 2 tbsp mirin
- 2 tbsp coriander, chopped
- 2 tbsp basil, chopped
- 2 tbsp oil
- 2 tbsp fish sauce

Directions

1. Place all ingredients, except the beef, salt and pepper, in a blender; process until smooth. Season the beef with salt and pepper. Place all in a zipper bag; shake well to combine. Marinate in the fridge for 4 hours.
2. Preheat the air fryer to 350 F. Place the beef in the air fryer and cook for 12 minutes, or more if you like it really well done. Let sit for a couple of minutes before serving. Serve with cooked rice and fresh veggies.

BASIC MEATLOAF

Cooking Time: 40 minutes
Serves: 8

Ingredients:

- 2 lbs. ground beef
- 1 shallot, chopped
- 2 eggs
- 3 garlic cloves minced
- 3 tablespoon tomato sauce
- 3 tablespoon parsley, chopped
- 3/4 cup Panko breadcrumbs
- 1/3 cup milk
- 1 ½ teaspoon salt or to taste

- 1 ½ teaspoon Italian seasoning
- ¼ teaspoon ground black pepper
- ½ teaspoon ground paprika

Directions:
1. Thoroughly mix ground beef with egg, onion, garlic, crumbs, and all the ingredients in a bowl.
2. Grease a meatloaf pan with oil or butter and spread the minced beef in the pan.
3. Press "Power Button" of Air Fry Oven and turn the dial to select the "Bake" mode.
4. Press the Time button and again turn the dial to set the cooking time to 40 minutes.
5. Now push the Temp button and rotate the dial to set the temperature at 375 degrees F.
6. Once preheated, place the beef baking pan in the oven and close its lid.
7. Slice and serve.

SAUCE GLAZED MEATLOAF

Cooking Time: 55 minutes
Serves: 4

Ingredients:
- 1 lb. ground beef
- ½ onion chopped
- 1 egg
- 1 ½ garlic clove, minced
- 1 ½ tablespoon ketchup
- 1 ½ tablespoon fresh parsley, chopped
- 1/4 cup breadcrumbs
- 2 tablespoons milk
- Salt to taste
- 1 ½ teaspoon herb seasoning
- ¼ teaspoon black pepper
- ½ teaspoon ground paprika

Glaze:

- 3/4 cup ketchup
- 1 ½ teaspoon white vinegar
- 2 ½ tablespoon brown sugar
- 1 teaspoon garlic powder
- ½ teaspoon onion powder
- ¼ teaspoon ground black pepper
- ¼ teaspoon salt

Directions:

1. Thoroughly mix ground beef with egg, onion, garlic, crumbs, and all the ingredients in a bowl.
2. Grease a meatloaf pan with oil or butter and spread the minced beef in the pan.
3. Press "Power Button" of Air Fry Oven and turn the dial to select the "Bake" mode.
4. Press the Time button and again turn the dial to set the cooking time to 40 minutes.
5. Now push the Temp button and rotate the dial to set the temperature at 375 degrees F.
6. Once preheated, place the beef baking pan in the oven and close its lid.
7. Meanwhile, prepare the glaze by whisking its ingredients in a saucepan.
8. Stir cook for 5 minutes until it thickens.
9. Brush this glaze over the meatloaf and bake it again for 15 minutes.
10. Slice and serve.

ZUCCHINI BEEF MEATLOAF

Cooking Time: 40 minutes
Serves: 8

Ingredients:
- 2 lbs. ground beef
- 1 cup zucchini, shredded
- 2 eggs
- 3 garlic cloves minced
- 3 tablespoon Worcestershire sauce
- 3 tablespoon fresh parsley, chopped

- 3/4 cup Panko breadcrumbs
- 1/3 cup beef broth
- Salt to taste
- ¼ teaspoon ground black pepper
- ½ teaspoon ground paprika

Directions:
1. Thoroughly mix ground beef with egg, zucchini, onion, garlic, crumbs, and all the ingredients in a bowl.
2. Grease a meatloaf pan with oil or butter and spread the minced beef in the pan.
3. Press "Power Button" of Air Fry Oven and turn the dial to select the "Bake" mode.
4. Press the Time button and again turn the dial to set the cooking time to 40 minutes.
5. Now push the Temp button and rotate the dial to set the temperature at 375 degrees F.
6. Once preheated, place the beef baking pan in the oven and close its lid.
7. Slice and serve.

CARROT BEEF CAKE

Cooking Time: 60 minutes
Serves: 10

Ingredients:
- 3 eggs, beaten
- 1/2 cup almond milk
- 1-oz. onion soup mix
- 1 cup dry bread crumbs
- 2 cups shredded carrots
- 2 lbs. lean ground beef
- 1/2-lb. ground pork

Directions:
1. Thoroughly mix ground beef with carrots and all other ingredients in a bowl.
2. Grease a meatloaf pan with oil or butter and spread the minced beef in the pan.

3. Press "Power Button" of Air Fry Oven and turn the dial to select the "Bake" mode.
4. Press the Time button and again turn the dial to set the cooking time to 60 minutes.
5. Now push the Temp button and rotate the dial to set the temperature at 350 degrees F.
6. Once preheated, place the beef baking pan in the oven and close its lid.
7. Slice and serve.

CRUMBLY OAT MEATLOAF

Cooking Time: 60 minutes
Serves: 8

Ingredients:
- 2 lbs. ground beef
- 1 cup of salsa
- 3/4 cup Quaker Oats
- 1/2 cup chopped onion
- 1 large egg, beaten
- 1 tablespoon Worcestershire sauce
- Salt and black pepper to taste

Directions:
1. Thoroughly mix ground beef with salsa, oats, onion, egg, and all the ingredients in a bowl.
2. Grease a meatloaf pan with oil or butter and spread the minced beef in the pan.
3. Press "Power Button" of Air Fry Oven and turn the dial to select the "Bake" mode.
4. Press the Time button and again turn the dial to set the cooking time to 60 minutes.
5. Now push the Temp button and rotate the dial to set the temperature at 350 degrees F.
6. Once preheated, place the beef baking pan in the oven and close its lid.
7. Slice and serve.

LIME GLAZED PORK KEBOBS

Cooking Time: 20 minutes
Serves: 6

Ingredients:

- 2 lb. pork, cubed
- 1/2 cup olive oil
- 1 lime juice
- 3 cloves garlic, minced
- 1 onion, sliced
- 1 teaspoon oregano, dried
- 1/4 teaspoon dried thyme,
- 1 teaspoon salt
- 1/4 teaspoon black pepper
- 1 tablespoon parsley, chopped
- 2 red pepper, cut into square
- 1 onion, cut into chunks

Directions:

1. Toss pork with the rest of the kebab ingredients in a bowl.
2. Cover the pork and marinate it for 30 minutes.
3. Thread the pork and veggies on the skewers alternately.
4. Place these pork skewers in the Air fry basket.
5. Press "Power Button" of Air Fry Oven and turn the dial to select the "Air fryer" mode.
6. Press the Time button and again turn the dial to set the cooking time to 20 minutes.
7. Now push the Temp button and rotate the dial to set the temperature at 370 degrees F.
8. Once preheated, place the Air fryer basket in the oven and close its lid.
9. Flip the skewers when cooked halfway through then resume cooking.
10. Serve warm.

PORK KEBAB TACOS

Cooking Time: 20 minutes
Serves: 6

Ingredients:
- Pork Kebabs
- 2 lbs. pork loin chops, diced
- 1 large onion, squares
- Salt, to taste

For the Wrap
- 6 burrito wraps
- 1/4 cup onions, sliced
- 1/2 cup tomatoes, sliced
- 1 1/2 cups romaine lettuce, chopped

Directions:
1. Toss pork and onion with salt in a bowl to season them.
2. Thread the pork and onion on the skewers alternately.
3. Place these pork skewers in the Air fry basket.
4. Press "Power Button" of Air Fry Oven and turn the dial to select the "Air fryer" mode.
5. Press the Time button and again turn the dial to set the cooking time to 20 minutes.
6. Now push the Temp button and rotate the dial to set the temperature at 370 degrees F.
7. Once preheated, place the Air fryer basket in the oven and close its lid.
8. Flip the skewers when cooked halfway through then resume cooking.
9. Place the warm burrito wrap on the serving plates.
10. Divide the tortilla ingredients on the tortillas and top them with pork kebabs.
11. Serve warm.

RAINBOW PORK SKEWERS

Cooking Time: 15 minutes

Serves: 4

Ingredients:
- 1-lb. boneless pork steaks, diced
- 1 eggplant, diced
- 1 yellow squash, diced
- 1 zucchini, diced
- 1/2 onion
- 4 slices ginger
- 5 cloves garlic
- 1 teaspoon cinnamon, ground
- 1 teaspoon cayenne
- 1 teaspoon salt

Directions:
1. Blend all the spices, ginger, garlic, and onion in a blender.
2. Toss the pork and veggies with prepared spice mixture then thread them over the skewers.
3. Marinate the spiced skewers for 30 minutes.
4. Place these pork skewers in the Air fry basket.
5. Press "Power Button" of Air Fry Oven and turn the dial to select the "Air fryer" mode.
6. Press the Time button and again turn the dial to set the cooking time to 15 minutes.
7. Now push the Temp button and rotate the dial to set the temperature at 350 degrees F.
8. Once preheated, place the Air fryer basket in the oven and close its lid.
9. Flip the skewers when cooked halfway through then resume cooking.
10. Serve warm.

TANGY PORK SAUSAGES

Cooking Time: 18 minutes
Serves: 4

Ingredients:

- ¾ lb. ground pork
- ¼ cup breadcrumbs
- ½ cup egg, beaten
- 1 teaspoon cumin
- 1 teaspoon paprika
- 1 teaspoon garlic powder
- 1 teaspoon onion powder
- ½ teaspoon cinnamon
- ½ teaspoon turmeric
- ½ teaspoon fennel seeds
- ½ teaspoon coriander seed, ground
- ½ teaspoon salt

Directions:
1. Mix pork mince with all the spices and kebab ingredients in a bowl.
2. Make 4 sausages out of this mixture and thread them on the skewers.
3. Refrigerate the pork skewers for 10 minutes to marinate.
4. Place these pork skewers in the Air fry basket.
5. Press "Power Button" of Air Fry Oven and turn the dial to select the "Air fryer" mode.
6. Press the Time button and again turn the dial to set the cooking time to 8 minutes.
7. Now push the Temp button and rotate the dial to set the temperature at 350 degrees F.
8. Once preheated, place the Air fryer basket in the oven and close its lid.
9. Flip the skewers when cooked halfway through then resume cooking.
10. Serve warm.

ROASTED PORK SHOULDER

Cooking Time: 1hr 30 minutes
Serves: 12

Ingredients:
- 6 lb. pork shoulder, boneless
- 8 cups buttermilk

Spice rub:
- 1 cup olive oil
- juice of 1 lemon
- 1 teaspoon thyme
- 5 teaspoon minced garlic
- Salt to taste
- Black pepper to taste

Directions:
1. Soak the pork shoulder in the buttermilk in a pot and cover to marinate.
2. Refrigerate the pork leg for 8 hours then remove it from the milk.
3. Place the pork shoulder in a baking tray.
4. Whisk spice rub ingredients in a bowl and brush over the pork liberally.
5. Press "Power Button" of Air Fry Oven and turn the dial to select the "Air Roast" mode.
6. Press the Time button and again turn the dial to set the cooking time to 1 hr. 30 minutes.
7. Now push the Temp button and rotate the dial to set the temperature at 370 degrees F.
8. Once preheated, place the pork baking tray in the oven and close its lid.
9. Serve warm.

DESSERTS RECIPES

CINNAMON BAKED APPLES WITH RAISINS & WALNUTS

Cooking Time: 35 minutes
Serves: 2

Ingredients:
- 2 granny smith apples, cored, bottom intact
- 2 tbsp butter, cold
- 3 tbsp sugar
- 3 tbsp crushed walnuts
- 2 tbsp raisins
- 1 tsp cinnamon

Directions
1. In a bowl, add butter, sugar, walnuts, raisins and cinnamon; mix with fingers until you obtain a crumble. Arrange the apples in the Air fryer. Stuff the apples with the filling mixture. Cook for 30 minutes at 400 F.

VANILLA CHOCOLATE BROWNIES WITH WALNUTS

Cooking Time: 35 minutes
Serves: 10

Ingredients:
- 6 oz dark chocolate
- 6 oz butter
- ¾ cup white sugar
- 3 eggs
- 2 tsp vanilla extract
- ¾ cup flour
- ¼ cup cocoa powder
- 1 cup chopped walnuts

- 1 cup white chocolate chips

Directions

1. Line a pan inside your Air fryer with baking paper. In a saucepan, melt chocolate and butter over low heat. Do not stop stirring until you obtain a smooth mixture. Let cool slightly, whisk in eggs and vanilla. Sift flour and cocoa and stir to mix well. Sprinkle the walnuts over and add the white chocolate into the batter. Pour the batter into the pan and cook for 20 minutes at 340 F. Serve with raspberry syrup and ice cream.

RASPBERRY CHOCOLATE CAKE

Cooking Time: 40 minutes
Serves: 8

Ingredients:

- 1 ½ cups flour
- ⅓ cup cocoa powder
- 2 tsp baking powder
- ¾ cup white sugar
- ¼ cup brown sugar
- ⅔ cup butter
- 2 tsp vanilla extract
- 1 cup milk
- 1 tsp baking soda
- 2 eggs
- 1 cup freeze-dried raspberries
- 1 cup chocolate chips

Directions

1. Line a cake tin with baking powder. In a bowl, sift flour, cocoa and baking powder. Place the sugars, butter, vanilla, milk and baking soda into a microwave-safe bowl and heat for 60 seconds until the butter melts and the ingredients incorporate; let cool slightly. Whisk the eggs into the mixture.
2. Pour the wet ingredients into the dry ones, and fold to combine. Add in the raspberries and chocolate chips into the batter. Pour the batter into the tin and

cook for 30 minutes at 350 F.

AMAZING MARSHMALLOWS PIE

Cooking Time: 10 minutes
Serves: 4

Ingredients:
- 4 graham cracker sheets, snapped in half
- 8 large marshmallows
- 8 squares each of dark, milk and white chocolate

Directions
1. Arrange the cracker halves on a board. Put 2 marshmallows onto half of the graham cracker halves. Place 2 squares of chocolate onto the cracker with the marshmallows. Put the remaining crackers on top to create 4 sandwiches. Wrap each one in the baking paper so it resembles a parcel. Cook in the fryer for 5 minutes at 340 F.

BANANA SPLIT

Cooking Time: 14 minutes
Serves: 8

Ingredients:
- 3 tablespoons coconut oil
- 1 cup panko breadcrumbs
- ½ cup corn flour
- 2 eggs
- 4 bananas, peeled and halved lengthwise
- 3 tablespoons sugar
- ¼ teaspoon ground cinnamon
- 2 tablespoons walnuts, chopped

Directions:

1. In a medium skillet, melt the coconut oil over medium heat and cook breadcrumbs for about 3-4 minutes or until golden browned and crumbled, stirring continuously.
2. Transfer the breadcrumbs into a shallow bowl and set aside to cool.
3. In a second bowl, place the corn flour.
4. In a third bowl, whisk the eggs.
5. Coat the banana slices with flour and then, dip into eggs and finally, coat evenly with the breadcrumbs.
6. In a small bowl, mix together the sugar and cinnamon.
7. Press "Power Button" of Air Fry Oven and turn the dial to select the "Air Fry" mode.
8. Press the Time button and again turn the dial to set the cooking time to 10 minutes.
9. Now push the Temp button and rotate the dial to set the temperature at 280 degrees F.
10. Press "Start/Pause" button to start.
11. When the unit beeps to show that it is preheated, open the lid.
12. Arrange the banana slices in "Air Fry Basket" and sprinkle with cinnamon sugar.
13. Insert the basket in the oven.
14. Transfer the banana slices onto plates to cool slightly
15. Sprinkle with chopped walnuts and serve.

CRISPY BANANA SLICES

Cooking Time: 15 minutes
Serves: 8

Ingredients:
- 4 medium ripe bananas, peeled
- 1/3 cup rice flour, divided
- 2 tablespoons all-purpose flour
- 2 tablespoons corn flour
- 2 tablespoons desiccated coconut
- ½ teaspoon baking powder
- ½ teaspoon ground cardamom
- Pinch of salt

- Water, as required
- ¼ cup sesame seeds

Directions:

1. In a shallow bowl, mix together 2 tablespoons of rice flour, all-purpose flour, corn flour, coconut, baking powder, cardamom, and salt.
2. Gradually, add the water and mix until a thick and smooth mixture forms.
3. In a second bowl, place the remaining rice flour.
4. In a third bowl, add the sesame seeds.
5. Cut each banana into half and then, cut each half in 2 pieces lengthwise.
6. Dip the banana slices into coconut mixture and then, coat with the remaining rice flour, followed by the sesame seeds.
7. Press "Power Button" of Air Fry Oven and turn the dial to select the "Air Fry" mode.
8. Press the Time button and again turn the dial to set the cooking time to 15 minutes.
9. Now push the Temp button and rotate the dial to set the temperature at 390 degrees F.
10. Press "Start/Pause" button to start.
11. When the unit beeps to show that it is preheated, open the lid.
12. Arrange the banana slices in "Air Fry Basket" and insert in the oven.
13. Transfer the banana slices onto plates to cool slightly
14. Transfer the banana slices onto plates to cool slightly before serving.

PINEAPPLE BITES

Cooking Time: 10 minutes
Serves: 4

Ingredients:

For Pineapple Sticks:
- ½ of pineapple
- ¼ cup desiccated coconut

For Yogurt Dip:
- 1 tablespoon fresh mint leaves, minced

- 1 cup vanilla yogurt

Directions:
1. Remove the outer skin of the pineapple and cut into long 1-2 inch thick sticks.
2. In a shallow dish place the coconut.
3. Coat the pineapple sticks with coconut evenly.
4. Press "Power Button" of Air Fry Oven and turn the dial to select the "Air Fry" mode.
5. Press the Time button and again turn the dial to set the cooking time to 10 minutes.
6. Now push the Temp button and rotate the dial to set the temperature at 390 degrees F.
7. Press "Start/Pause" button to start.
8. When the unit beeps to show that it is preheated, open the lid.
9. Arrange the pineapple sticks in lightly greased "Air Fry Basket" and insert in the oven.
10. Meanwhile, for dip in a bowl, mix together mint and yogurt.
11. Serve pineapple sticks with yogurt dip.

CHEESECAKE BITES

Cooking Time: 2 minutes
Serves: 12

Ingredients:
- 8 oz. cream cheese, softened
- ½ cup plus 2 tablespoons sugar, divided
- 4 tablespoons heavy cream, divided
- ½ teaspoon vanilla extract
- ½ cup almond flour

Directions:
1. In a bowl of a stand mixer, fitted with paddle attachment, add the cream cheese, ½ cup of sugar, 2 tablespoons of heavy cream and vanilla extract and beat until smooth.
2. With a scooper, scoop the mixture onto a parchment paper-lined baking pan.

3. Freeze for about 30 minutes or until firm.
4. In a small bowl, place the remaining cream.
5. In another small bowl, add the almond flour and remaining sugar and mix well.
6. Dip each cheesecake bite in cream and then coat with the flour mixture.
7. Press "Power Button" of Air Fry Oven and turn the dial to select the "Air Fry" mode.
8. Press the Time button and again turn the dial to set the cooking time to 2 minutes.
9. Now push the Temp button and rotate the dial to set the temperature at 300 degrees F.
10. Press "Start/Pause" button to start.
11. When the unit beeps to show that it is preheated, open the lid.
12. Arrange the pan in "Air Fry Basket" and insert in the oven.
13. Serve warm.

CHOCOLATE BITES

Cooking Time: 13 minutes
Serves: 8

Ingredients:
- 2 cups plain flour
- 2 tablespoons cocoa powder
- ½ cup icing sugar
- Pinch of ground cinnamon
- 1 teaspoon vanilla extract
- ¾ cup chilled butter
- ¼ cup chocolate, chopped into 8 chunks

Directions:
1. In a bowl, mix together the flour, icing sugar, cocoa powder, cinnamon and vanilla extract.
2. With a pastry cutter, cut the butter and mix till a smooth dough forms.
3. Divide the dough into 8 equal-sized balls.
4. Press 1 chocolate chunk in the center of each ball and cover with the dough completely.

5. Place the balls into the baking pan.
6. Press "Power Button" of Air Fry Oven and turn the dial to select the "Air Fry" mode.
7. Press the Time button and again turn the dial to set the cooking time to 8 minutes.
8. Now push the Temp button and rotate the dial to set the temperature at 355 degrees F.
9. Press "Start/Pause" button to start.
10. When the unit beeps to show that it is preheated, open the lid.
11. Arrange the pan in "Air Fry Basket" and insert in the oven.
12. After 8 minutes of cooking, set the temperature at 320 degrees F for 5 minutes.
13. Place the baking pan onto the wire rack to cool completely before serving.

SHORTBREAD FINGERS

Cooking Time: 12 minutes
Serves: 10

Ingredients:
- 1/3 cup caster sugar
- 1 2/3 cups plain flour
- ¾ cup butter

Directions:
1. In a large bowl, mix together the sugar and flour.
2. Add the butter and mix until a smooth dough forms.
3. Cut the dough into 10 equal-sized fingers.
4. With a fork, lightly prick the fingers.
5. Place the fingers into the lightly greased baking pan.
6. Press "Power Button" of Air Fry Oven and turn the dial to select the "Air Fry" mode.
7. Press the Time button and again turn the dial to set the cooking time to 12 minutes.
8. Now push the Temp button and rotate the dial to set the temperature at 355 degrees F.
9. Press "Start/Pause" button to start.

10. When the unit beeps to show that it is preheated, open the lid.
11. Arrange the pan in "Air Fry Basket" and insert in the oven.
12. Place the baking pan onto a wire rack to cool for about 5-10 minutes.
13. Now, invert the short bread fingers onto wire rack to completely cool before serving.

BERRY TACOS

Cooking Time: 5 minutes
Serves: 2

Ingredients:
- 2 soft shell tortillas
- 4 tablespoons strawberry jelly
- ¼ cup fresh blueberries
- ¼ cup fresh raspberries
- 2 tablespoons powdered sugar

Directions:
1. Spread 2 tablespoons of strawberry jelly over each tortilla
2. Top each with berries evenly and sprinkle with powdered sugar.
3. Press "Power Button" of Air Fry Oven and turn the dial to select the "Air Fry" mode.
4. Press the Time button and again turn the dial to set the cooking time to 5 minutes.
5. Now push the Temp button and rotate the dial to set the temperature at 300 degrees F.
6. Press "Start/Pause" button to start.
7. When the unit beeps to show that it is preheated, open the lid.
8. Arrange the tortillas in "Air Fry Basket" and insert in the oven.
9. Serve warm.

CPSIA information can be obtained
at www.ICGtesting.com
Printed in the USA
BVHW061131080121
597269BV00008B/482